FUNDAMENTALS OF
BUILDING COMPONENTS
AND SYSTEMS
For Community Association Managers

DENIS RUDNEV

authorHOUSE®

AuthorHouse™
1663 Liberty Drive
Bloomington, IN 47403
www.authorhouse.com
Phone: 1 (800) 839-8640

Published by AuthorHouse 05/22/2017

ISBN: 978-1-5246-6056-7 (sc)
ISBN: 978-1-5246-6055-0 (e)

Library of Congress Control Number: 2017902109

Print information available on the last page.

Preface

This work is intended to help community association managers and other staff members to better understand the physical components of properties they manage. Unfortunately, few technical references exist in the industry that is aimed at helping community association managers understand the basics of HVAC or Elevator systems from the prospective of community association management. The bulk of what is available is highly technical in nature and is geared for a trade specific audience. So, I have aimed this work at an audience of my peers and those who are aspiring to enter the industry.

I hope that this work will assist in providing a basic understanding of building components. This foundation is the most important step since it will allow the knowledge of where to look for answers, which questions to ask and for a more professional way to communicate.

Additionally, I hope to inspire my peers to innovate and add to this young industry with the hope that the next generations of professionals be a much more prepared to make the right decisions. This is needed because our communities are becoming more and more complex with the developments in technology and will eventually require a higher level of technical skills than demanded today.

Contents

Landscape Maintenance

The purpose of any maintenance program is to maximize an asset's useful life. With landscaping, it is important to understand that one is dealing with an asset that is comprised of living organisms. Turf, trees, palms and ornamental plants, for example; reproduce, need nutrient, sun and grooming to meet their respective life spans without the need for premature replacement.

This guide will bring to your attention basic concepts and issues relevant to a community's landscape management needs. Regardless of H.O.A. or Condominium style associations the basic presented criteria remains constant. Presented concepts will however vary in quantity and complexity depending on the physical nature of the property.

1. Landscape Maintenance Contract
2. Turf Maintenance
3. Palm Maintenance
4. Tree Maintenance
5. Ornamental Plant Maintenance
6. Mulch
7. Landscaping Design

Landscape Maintenance Contract:

The basic idea behind all landscape maintenance contracts is to preserve the established standards of existing landscaping. The contractor will agree to provide the man power and equipment to accomplish a uniformed look of the existing plant material and to remove debris generated by the work.

The typical composition of the scope of work is as follows:

Service Visits:

Service visits vary based upon the needs of an individual community, they may range from keeping a full-time crew on the property every day which is possible in very large H.O.A. style communities with miles of privacy hedge and dozens of acres of turf to once a monthly or by-monthly service if the scope of work is limited to a small planter bed at the entrance to the community.

An average service schedule will range from by-weekly 26 services to 36 services adjusted to suit the seasonal growth rates of the plant material. The seasonal adjustment is needed due to the drastic increase in growth of the plant life during summer months and nearly dormant state during the winter. Considering the seasons, it is of benefit to the community to manage services accordingly. Fox example, if the community is serviced 34 times per year it may want to consider 2 services from January through March, 3 services from April to May, 4 services from June through August, 3 services September though October, and 2 from November through December. This seasonal adjustment will meet the typical service visit needs for South Florida but may be further adjusted to other locations depending on the inherent weather patterns.

Mowing:

Mowing of turf typically occur every service visit. The work is done utilizing appropriate equipment for the scope of work ranging from 60" (60" width that is covered by the mover blades) commercial sit down mowers to small walk behind mowers needed for narrow strips of turf. The focus is to maintain the height of grass blades at an acceptable and uniformed level. Typically, the mower blades are set at 2". The setting can be adjusted higher but lower settings may cause bald spots where bumps are found in the ground.

Edging:

Edging is the practice of creating a defined edge to the turf areas. This is performed with an "edger" which is a hand-held tool that is ran along the outer perimeter of the turf area cutting away excess grass that is over growing on to paved or other surfaces not intended for turf.

Weed Control:

Basic maintenance contract including weed control will not include weeds in the turf, this is a separate service, but it includes controlling weeds in the garden beds within pavers, tree rings, exterior walkways and vehicle driveways. The contract will typically mention the methods that are used; including chemical, mechanical and hand removal. The contactor will select the best method for each maintained location. For example, the pool deck will most likely be treated chemically with a weed killer and areas such as planter beds with seasonal annuals will be de-weeded by hand due to the sensitive nature of these plants.

Hedging:

Hedging is a practice commonly evolves the use of a "hedger" to shape the ornamental hedge rows and designs within the landscaping. The contractor's objective is to achieve uniformity in the appearance of the hedge and to prevent overgrowth that could have a negative impact on the design. Not all materials used in landscape design are intended for hedging. It is important to be clear with the landscape maintenance contractor as to what needs to be hedged and what does not. For example; ferns and some flowering hedges may not be suited for hedging due to the intention within design. Additionally, plants such as ferns have a dramatically worse appearance after hedging compared to their natural look.

Trees and Palms:

Trees and palms as part of regular scope of work in landscape maintenance are typically depended on height. Palm tops reachable by a pole saw (12'-14' in height) typically will be tended to by removal of the seed pods and dead and unsightly fronds. Trees are typically tended to by removal of branches that may be an obstacle for walkways no higher than 8'-10' from the ground. The basic idea for tree maintenance is to allow for unobstructed pedestrian passage. Additionally, tree trunks are tended to by removal of "suckers" which are sprouts growing out of the trunk, again, within the 8'-10' height criteria.

Debris Removal:

During the process of maintenance debris that is naturally occurring and debris that is produced due to maintenance work needs to be removed. Litter is also considered debris. First step involved within this process is managing the debris in to one location for pick up. This is achieved either by hand, rake or blower. Blowers are commonly utilized to clear walkways and driveways as well as other open areas. It is recommended that debris not be blown into the shrubbery as if sweeping dust under the rug because an accumulated debris lair will serve as a host to insects and other pests. Instead the landscape workers will need to remove all debris from underneath the plant material and haul it off location.

Turf Maintenance:

Maintenance of turf areas consists of regular shaping by way of mowing and edging as well as feeding the turf through fertilization and watering. Additionally, turf areas must be protected from pests, diseases to be replaced by disease same in multiple locations and weeds that can create unsightly dead and damaged locations.

The routine shaping of the turf areas as applicable to the regular scope of work will allow for uniformity. This practice is typically done every service visit with use of mechanical equipment as earlier discussed.

Palm Maintenance:

The basic scope of palm maintenance that may or may not be included in the general scope of work of the landscape maintenance agreement consists of 3 parts: Cleaning, Fertilization and diseases control.

Cleaning of the palm is a practice of cutting away of dead fronds and seed pods, and is typically done once a year before the beginning of hurricane season. According to the Broward County regulation (currently one of a minority of counties requiring licensing to perform palm cleaning) the basic criteria is as follows:

Only brown fronds are subject to removal, cutting away of green fronds may cause damage to the palm. Fronds must be cut as close to the trunk as possible using a saw producing a clean cut. Ripping or tearing of the fronds may cause harm to the palm not to mention the esthetical damage. Frond removal must not exceed what is called the "10 and 2 o'clock" rule which dictates that only those fronds that are hanging below the horizontal line with the ground are eligible for removal. Occasionally partial palm trimming is necessary multiple times a year. In some cases, tree trimming is a separate contract. Fertilization is done with a slow release (granular) palm fertilizer a minimum of two times per year with quarterly fertilization being ideal. A granular slow release palm fertilizer contains roughly 8% to 9 % Nitrogen, 2% to 3% Phosphorus, 11% to 12% Potassium and trace elements. Because palms are highly prone to several potentially fatal micronutrient deficiencies, any fertilizer applied to them should contain 1-2% Iron and Manganese, plus trace amounts of Zinc, Copper, and Boron to prevent these deficiencies. This is commercially available with NPK ratios of (12-4-12) or (8-2-12). The "N-P-K" ratio reflects the available nutrients —by weight—contained in that fertilizer, and is clearly displayed on product packaging regardless of brand.

The key aspect of decease control for palm trees is adequate fertilization and quick notice of potential for problems with the palm. By providing a palm tree with quality fertilizer the palm remains strong and healthy by being able to fight off decease, however there are some deceases that may not be curable and loss of the palm tree is inevitable. Monitoring of palm trees and timely treatment for decease or nutrient deficiencies is the main factor in protecting palm trees. The best sign to look for when determining the condition of any palm tree is the visual condition of the heart. The heart of the palm tree is the green top from which fronds grow. When the top or the heart is a healthy green color without visible change in texture or shape and new fronds are developing without obvious abnormalities then the palm tree is healthy and strong. However, yellowing in the upper frond canopy, wilting, frond disfigurement and frond curling is a sign of decease or malnutrition that warrants a consultation from a qualified landscaper or pest control specialist.

Tree Maintenance

Trees or Hardwood trees to distinguish from palms require generally minimal maintenance aside from pruning. Furthermore, pruning of trees dues not generally occur every year. A tree may need pruning for several reasons which may be to thin the crown to permit new growth or allow better air lifting circulation in preparation for hurricane season, to reduce the height of the tree and to prevent the tree from becoming an obstacle either to the line of sight, nearby property or in the form of obstructing lower branched to pedestrians. Please note that toping of tree is not tree is not permitted.

Existing guide lines in Broward County emphasize tree pruning techniques aiming at retaining the natural shape of the tree. Removals of limbs and branches must promote the natural growth pattern. This means that the pruning technique must aim at retaining one straight center mass trunk. Trees must retain a pyramid like appearance within the canopy that allow for maximum capture of sunlight.

Avoid hacking which is the removal of most of the foliage from the tree not only due to the poor esthetic standards effect but also because of the degrading physical condition of the tree. Over lifting is another pruning malpractice that must be avoided. Over lifting occurs by removing majority of the foliage from the bottom making the tree top heavy. Ironically, over lifting typically occurs during hurricane pruning projects and completely defeats the point of the project by producing a tree with a heavy and unbalanced top.

Ornamental Plant Maintenance:

Nearly all existing ornamental plants in the landscape require maintenance to stay healthy and attractive. Regular pruning, season appropriate watering, fertilization and pest control are all part of a good landscape management program.

Some plants are more demanding in care than others, for example, annual plants such as impatiens demand more water than the more durable shrubs and ornamental grasses. Annuals last a growing season. South Florida with multiple seasons will require annuals to be replaced at beginning of each cycle. Rotating different species of annuals to match growing seasons will maximize life cycle. Prefer native perennials inside flower beds. Additionally, some plants, such as roses have high fertilization needs and disease control.

On the other hand, plants such as ornamental grasses, green island fichus and junipers, when properly planted on a good site, require little care once established and are considered good low-maintenance plants.

Caring for ornamental plants is more difficult when they are not well-suited to the site selected or when they are improperly planted. Azaleas, for instance, prefer a moist, well-drained soil and shade from the mid-afternoon sun. Most ornamental plant materials have varying tolerances needs to sun, shade, and watering and soil chemistry.

Pruning of established plant material will allow for new growth and better rate of flowering, additionally, pruning will remove unsightly dead stems of plants. Watering of ornamental material also plays a pivotal role in the health of the landscape. Adjusting watering times to meet seasonal demand is vital. The plant material metabolic rate is higher in the warm temperatures and lower in the cold. Warmer temperatures allow and encourage the plant to absorb more water which in turn stimulates a lot of growth. Colder temperatures slow the metabolic rate of plant material leading to slower absorption by the root system, intern this can lead to plant materials being exposed to fungus and rot. Rule of thumb is the colder the climate the less water the plant must receive.

Fertilization is important for healthy plant growth; therefore, fertilizing during the growth periods of the plant yields the best results. Prime growth periods as mentioned are the warmer months of the year, ranging between May and September. Additionally, fertilization during the warmer months will allow plant to be more resistant to pests and decease. Pest control for ornamental plants should be performed on a regular basis. Preventative treatments will safeguard the plants from pest and decease attacks that are inevitable in warm climate such as in Florida.

Mulch:

Mulching of the planted beds is an esthetically and functionally beneficial step in landscape maintenance. Its functionality is defined by the mulch's ability to act as a protective shield for the landscaping. The benefits include: Act of mulching prevent loss of water from the soil through evaporation. Mulches reduce the growth of weeds, when the mulch material itself is weed-free and applied deeply enough to prevent weed germination or to smother existing weeds. Mulching keeps the soil cooler in the temperatures and warmer in cold temperatures, thus maintaining a more even soil temperature.

Mulching prevents soil splashing, which not only stops erosion but keeps soil-borne diseases from splashing up onto the plants. Decaying mulch also adds nutrients to the soil. Mulching prevent crusting of the soil surface, thus improving the absorption and movement of water into the soil. Mulches prevent the trunks of trees and shrubs from damage by landscape maintenance equipment. There are many mulching practices ranging from organic to plastic alternatives.

Most common are mulches made from chipped wood. They are most commonly available in red, yellow, black or natural colors. Installation is between 2" to 3" thick. Avoid purchasing mulch that is priced extremely below market rate because this could serve as a sign that the mulch has been manufactured with substandard material like diseased trees that can infect the plant life after installation. Substandard material also causes harmful toxins to be absorbed by soil.

Landscape design and installation:

Designing a new landscape is a science as well as an art. First consideration is to be sure that there is sufficient irrigation coverage for the intended landscape area. This is determined with a run of the sprinkler system (Wet Check) which will show how the water is distributed throughout the area. Inadequate coverage must be adjusted or repaired before the installation since newly installed plants will need water right away.

Second is the consideration of sun exposure of the landscaping area. All plants have specific tolerances to light conditions which range from the need for full sun to only shade.

Third consider the plants to be used with the intended design. Within this consideration one must be mindful of growth rate and maximum maintained height, light/ shade tolerance and growth pattern, dues the plant run along the ground surface like a ground cover or dues it grows up and out like a shrub or spreads buds to the sides of the plant like a Bromeliad. With the available software that is on the market, it is a good idea to request a digital rendering from the installer with the intended design.

Striving towards sustainability in landscape design is one idea can prove prudent for the future. In landscape, sustainability can be defined by using plant that have high tolerances, low watering needs and that generate "pups" though this lifecycle. Most Bromeliads for example, generate pups as part of their reproduction allowing for separation from the parent plant and replanting back in to the landscape resulting in savings. Other plants such as Mother In-Law Tongue and Ground Orchid, just to name a few, have similar reproductive means and feature high tolerances with low maintenance requirements. Sustainability also requires proper drainage, percolation of water, proper irrigation heads installed at proper heights to accommodate changing plat tiers.

In general terms, landscape design should not only have a "Wow" effect right after the installation, but must be lasting and easy to maintain. By following this rule, not only will the result be visually appealing, but also cost effective.

Paved Surfaces Maintenance

Because of the constant impact from natural elements and use, all pavements require maintenance and repair. There are many factors that impact a paved surface causing it to deteriorate; traffic loads, temperature (causing expansion with heat and contraction with cold), water and object impact, such as heavy objects placed on the surface. Although it is a regular cycle of stresses for the paved surface over time without a regular maintenance plan the damage can have a significant negative impact on the useful life of the paved surface.

It is easy for most individuals to see when a paved surface needs repair and maintenance. The obvious pot holes, cracking and water puddles give away the fact of deteriorated condition. However as easy as it is to spot that a problem exists it is difficult to determine what must be done to remedy it for an untrained person. This manual is intended to identify and give a basic perimeter for resolution of problems and to provide an outline for an effective maintenance program.

Paved Surface System

The paved surface system, be it in the form of a parking lot or a roadway consists of top level of pavement and foundation materials. The foundation is composed of Subbase and Subgrage levels which support the pavement. Subbase is a granular (gravel) lair of a specified material installed to a designed thickness. This lair is installed on top of Subgrade which is naturally accruing surfaces such as soils which are prepared to a typical 12" thickness of resistance. The below diagram illustrates a typical structure which should be considered always when maintaining or repairing paved surfaces.

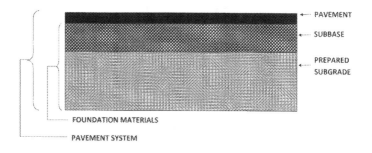

Left bracket labels: FOUNDATION MATERIALS / PAVEMENT SYSTEM
Right labels: PAVEMENT / SUBBASE / PREPARED SUBGRADE

Drainage

Single most important element in functionality and useful life of a paved surface, be it a parking lot or a road way, is drainage. Water has an impact on the surface of pavement, but the most dramatic and costly impact is on the sub lair below the pavement. Water intrusion beneath the pavement, most commonly caused by improper drainage reduces the ability of soil to withstand stresses. Although pavement lair absorbs much of the traffic stress of everyday use, ultimately, however, stress is transmitted to the foundation lair of soils and sands. An accumulation of sub surface water underneath pavement will greatly reduce the ability of the sub surface layer to withstand stress. In turn, the inability to withstand stress will lead to deformation of surface areas allowing for water accumulation and surface deterioration.

Maintaining and repairing drainage system will prevent water intrusion into the sub surface lairs. A properly designed will allow for water to be directed in to the storm water drains and dispersed off the property before it has a chance to penetrate the sub lairs. The factor that plays the most important role in this process is proper grading of the lot or roadway that leads water flow directly to catch basins.

In maintaining the drainage system, the first step is to keep it free of obstruction in the piping. Jetting and vacuuming at 3-5 year intervals will remove buildup of silt and debris allowing for a smoother flow of water away from property. If the issue of surface water accumulation results from water not flowing directly in to the drains, then grading should be examined as an option.

Surface Condition Evaluation

As in any maintenance program careful planning of maintenance and routine inspection of the paved property is the key to prolonging useful life. As an initial step in evaluation paved assets is the inspection of all paved parking lots and roadways for surface condition, structural strength and drainage.

Paved surface inspection is best accomplished on foot rather than from a slow-moving automobile or a golf cart. By performing the inspection on foot one will be able to notice more relevant condition factors which could otherwise be overlooked. During the inspection, it is important to not only find a problem, but to also determine the cause of the problem, so that the repair that is performed will not reoccur in the future if the cause is corrected as well. For example; if a tree root is causing a crack in the pavement, patching the crack alone will not completely resolve the issue. To resolve the issue completely the root must either be severed or removed completely in addition to the crack patching.

It is recommended to maintain an inspection log or layout plan on which problems or defects are marked. This will allow for consistency and a firmer grasp on the overall condition of the asset and will help to determine the need for future repairs and maintenance.

Signs of Disrepair

Pavements in need of repair and maintenance can exhibit any or all the following deteriorations listed below:

Raveling:

This deterioration is evident by the aggregate particles progressively separating from surface of the pavement down ward. This is usually the first sign of deterioration apparent on a paved surface. The surface lairs begin to separate leaving a coarse "pock marked" appearance to the affected area. This is a progressive process of deterioration and over time leads to larger and larger particles to be broken away leaving a jagged surface that is inherent to erosion. Raveling typically occurs due to installation of pavement during inappropriate seasonal conditions, mostly cold or wet conditionals. Additionally, raveling may result from installation flaws such is poor mix design of the asphalt and prolonged traffic stresses without regular maintenance.

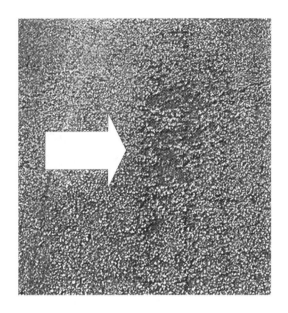

Alligator Cracks/ Cracking:

This form of deterioration manifests itself in a serious of connected cracks that define separated blocks surface over a section of the pavement that resembles an alligator skin. This deterioration is commonly caused due to over bending of the surface over unstable subgrade or lower lairs of pavement. The damaged sections of pavement are usually not large, but in some cases, can be if the paved surface is used to carry loads over the maximum allotted.

Upheaval:

This deterioration is identified by localized upward dislodgment of pavement. In warm climates, this condition signifies an accumulation of moisture in the subgrade soils or a force such as growing plant life pulls up the pavement. In cold climate locations, due to common effective cause being the swelling of the sub grade due to ice.

Pot Holes:

This is one of the most evident deteriorations that are defined by the emergence of craters in the pavement. Pot holes are typically the result of lack of maintenance or poor design of the pavement. Combined with traffic stress and the natural conditions improperly maintained or poorly installed surfaces will develop various forms of deteriorations eventually leading to pot holes. This defect is progressive and will increase in size and severity over time.

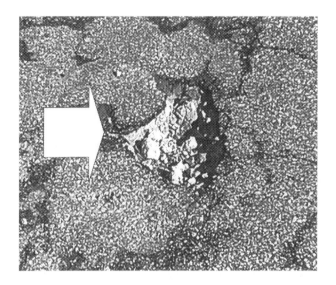

Grade Depressions:

Grade depressions are evident by localized depressed areas of paved surface. The depression can occur without cracking. This condition is frequently caused by settlement of the lower levels of pavement construction, poor construction or higher than intended loads.

Regular Maintenance and Repair

Below is a listing of condition circumstances and means of maintenance of repair. Although all maintenance and repairs of pavements have their own specifics the general approach is the same.

Good Condition of Paved Surface:

A paved surface in good condition will show minimal signs of deterioration. Some of the more common occurrences of deterioration are light cracking and light raveling that is caused by regular weather conditions and use. In a continuing effort to maintain the paved surface in a good condition apply seal coat to the surface every 3-5years. A sealcoat is a thin asphalt treatment that is utilized to waterproof and improves the texture of the surface.

Most common seal approach is for sealing of aged and lightly deteriorated asphalt with what is called a Fog Seal. A fog seal is a light application of slow-setting blended asphalt which is diluted with water. This method will have a rejuvenating effect on the surface and will seal small cracks. This seal is applied through spraying at the rate of 0.1 to 0.15 Gal per square yard. The rate of application is very important, because if the rate of application is too light than cracks within the surface will not be adequately sealed and too heavy an application will impair the skid resistance of the surface. Additional considerations must be made for curing time of the seal. This seal will take several hours to dry and therefore alterative parking locations and traffic routs must be arranged. Spraying of this seal must also make one mindful of protecting surfaces such as walls and curbs form occasional overspray.

Moderate Deterioration of Paved Surface:

This level of deterioration is characterized by existence of larger crack of approximately 0.5 inches in width and some raveling of asphalt. The cracks must first be prepared for repairs which include removing all weeds and debris from the cracks and applying herbicide to locations where weed growth is expected. The cracks are then commonly sealed with emulsified asphalt slurry or a fine grade of liquid asphalt mixed with sand. Fine cracks of 1/8 of an inch in width can be overlooked is a seal coat is to follow. For the few larger cracks one can utilize a fine sand-asphalt hot mix. After all the cracks on the surface have been tended to the paved surface should be over sprayed with a seal coat.

High Level of Deterioration:

This level of deterioration will display cracking, pot holes, raveling and depressions. A highly deteriorated paved surface can exhibit all or one extensive example of disrepair. Regardless of the combination having extensive damage to the paved surface warrants immediate attention.

The first step in repairing high levels of deterioration is to deal with areas of localized distress such as pot holes and deep cracking. The usual approach is to apply what is called a full depth asphalt patch. This approach includes the removal of the damaged surface and base as deep as necessary going down at least 4 inches in depth or until firm supporting base is reached. The width of the removed damaged surface must span at least a foot in to undamaged asphalt in a square or rectangular shape.

The next step is to compact the subgrade until it is firm and unyielding. If excessive water is the root of the damage consider drainage to drain water away in the future. After the subsurface is well compacted a bonding agent is applied to the edges of the square or rectangular cut. A bonding agent will allow the new asphalt to adhere to the old, undamaged. Then the cut is filled with hot dense graded plant-mix asphalt with each asphalt layer densely compacted with scope appropriate equipment. Following the completion localized distress repairs smaller cracks should be filled.

Grade depressed areas should be repaired and leveled. Specific attention must be given to proper grading or the slope that will allow for proper water runoff. Grade depressed areas may need larger amounts of fill and wider repair areas based on the amount of deterioration and depth of depression.

After the localized repairs to cracking raveling and grade depressions have been done it is highly recommended that an overlay of 1' inch of asphalt be installed of the paved surface sealed.

Please note that the instruction in this guide focuses on the general approach to maintaining and repairing paved surfaces and dues not factor materials and approach methods used locally for certain conditions. It is important to obtain several qualified opinions and repair estimates and then compare to determine the true scope of work or as an alternative obtain the services of a licensed Civil Engineer.

Domestic Plumbing System

Domestic plumbing in a residential building serves two purposes, providing fresh water for use and providing waste and storm water disposal. The plumbing system is an assembly of pipes, fittings, valves and fixtures that channel the movement of water or waste. These systems are a major part of any dwelling and demand a high degree of skill and craftsmanship due to the destructive nature of water that these systems facilitate. Major repairs to plumbing must be performed by a licensed plumber with experience in working on similar projects in order to avoid damage caused by errors during the performance of work. This guide will introduce some of the basic components of domestic plumbing systems as they relate to multi- residential buildings.

Domestic Water Supply Quality:

In nearly all circumstances in the United States the quality of the domestic water is heavily monitored by Federal, State, County and City authorities. Water used by the public is treated and supplied in a manner fit for consumption and immediate efforts are taken to advice the public of any instances where additional steps are needed for safe consumption such as the "Boil Water" advisement.

However, periodic quality concerns will arise. Most frequently it is the taste of chlorine in the water coming out of the tap. This is caused by small quantities of chlorine being injected into the water supply during treatment. Chlorine acts as a disinfectant and a safeguard against viral and bacterial contamination. This is most commonly noted in residences in near proximity to the water treatment plant. Chlorine dissipates quickly over time; therefore, residences at the further points from the treatment facility will have lower instances of the taste and smell of chlorine reported.

Local Drinking Water Quality Reports are available on the U.S. Environmental Protection Agency website at http://water.epa.gov/drink/local/.

Domestic Water Supply:

Domestic water supply refers to the water used in all circumstances by the dwelling inhabitants daily ranging from shower use to the use of washing machine and kitchen tap. Domestic water is provided by the local municipality and enters the building through the domestic cold water main line. This main line is terminated at a curb stop and then is connected to the water meter that provides consumption data to the provider. Immediately after the house meter is the backflow preventer and the main line shut-off valve. The main domestic water shut-off valve is used to completely shut all domestic water to the building. This shut-off valve is separate from fire sprinkler shut-off valve which is designated in red in contract to the blue of the domestic water shut-off valve.

The water entering the building from the municipal supplier has only enough pressure to reach between three to five stories upward to the end user. Therefore, in all instances of tall building construction mechanical equipment is used to provide adequate pressure to elevate the water up and to maintain adequate pressure. Adequate pressure is considered to be between 40-80 psi (Pounds per Square Inch). The lower pressure of the spectrum is noted during high water use periods. Additionally, for most equipment utilizing domestic water such as clothes and dish washers the minimum optimum pressure is 40 psi.

Domestic Water Pumps:

In lifting water above the level of the mainline results in a loss 1 pound per square inch of pressure every 2.3 feet of vertical elevation in any structure. This problem is solved by pressure boosting pumps that are installed at the ground level of a building. The pumps are fed by the main water supply line. There are several types of water pressure boosting pumps. Starting with systems of lower utilization such as elevated gravity tanks that have water pumped into a water tank located on the roof from which water is distributed by way of gravity to Hydropneumatic tank systems than pump water in to a pressure tank and then use pressurized air for upward distribution. Most common pumps used are constant speed and variable speed tankless pumps. These pumps take the direct feed of water from the main city line and elevate it directly to the end user through the building piping. In general, all pumps are constant pressure pump, meaning that the objective of the pump is to maintain a steady suitable flow level for the end user. Variable speed pump systems modulate the flow based on need. However, the types of the pump; constant or variable speed differ in cost of use, efficiency and mode of operation.

Typical Domestic Water Pump Set

Constant Speed Pump Systems:

Constant speed pump systems comprise of several pumps that are utilized to provide domestic water to the end user. At a minimum two pumps must be utilized in this system. The main or what is referred to as the lead pump is in constant use providing minimum required flow to the end user. The secondary or the lag pump is utilized to contribute additional flow during periods of increased demand. Depending on the size and height of the structure as well its design and size of the water main varying combinations of constant speed pumps may be utilized.

Variable Speed Pump Systems:

Variable speed pumps differ from constant speed pumps in the way that the speed of the motor or its ability to deliver flow rate of the water supply can be varied depending on demand. Only one variable speed pump can be used at a minimum. However, for large and frequently complex structures several variable speed pumps are used to obtain the same basic effect as those systems utilizing constant speed pumps. The presumed benefit for utilizing variable speed pump systems is that the speed of the motor is automatically adjusted to suit demand having a direct impact on energy consumption as opposed to the constant speed pump systems that require at least one pump running on a constant basis regardless of demand.

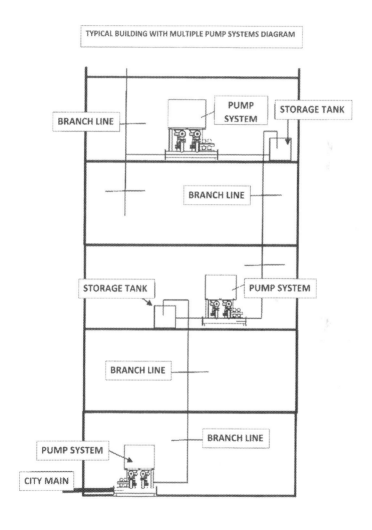

TYPICAL BUILDING WITH MULTIPLE PUMP SYSTEMS DIAGRAM

Piping:

From the pump room where the domestic water supply provided by the municipal authority is pressurized to be delivered to the elevated end user water travels through an assortment of pipes and valves that control the delivery at safe pressures. Domestic water supply is delivered up to the end user through copper piping that can be distinguished by its bronze color. Vertical stacks are installed running up through the slabs of the building floors branching out to the specific fixtures.

One of the most common problems related to piping is the effect that is commonly referred to as water hammering. Water hammering or Hydrostatic Shock is described as a hammering sound coming from the water supply pipes. This effect is caused by excessive building water pressure and poorly supported water supply piping. Additionally, certain valves may be a cause of water hammering if the flow is shut off excessively fast. Finally, water hammer noise suppression device or air riser arrestors absorb the shock of change in water direction when water is suddenly shut off may be missing or an old air chamber is filled with water.

Shut-Off Valves:

Shut-off valves are installed in most critical sections of the water supply design and range from the main shut-off valve to the branch line shut off that supplies water to a single dwelling or even the shut-off valve supplying water to a single fixture. For maintenance purposes those valves that control the flow of water to specific sections must be clearly marked and inspected. It is critical in case of a flood to be able to quickly find and shut off the line that is causing the flood.

Plumbing Insulation:

Plumbing line insulation and its components are major considerations in the design and installation of the plumbing and piping systems of multi-residential buildings. Insulation is used to minimize heat or cooling temperature loss through pipe, lower the appearance of condensation, keep piping lines safe to the touch, and reduce noise. Further insulation improves esthetics of exposed piping and protects the piping from potential damage.

Plumbing Fixtures:

Indoor plumbing exists only for supporting plumbing fixtures. Each fixture is designed for a specific function to provide water and maintain sanitary conditions, such as discharging used water from a kitchen sink or carrying away waste. Some of the numerous plumbing fixtures used in plumbing systems are water closets and urinals, showerheads, faucets, drinking fountains, bidets, floor drains, and emergency eyewashes, and washing machines. Plumbing fixtures are connected to the plumbing system piping by wide variety of fittings that regulate flow or perform functions needed to support the proper operation of the system.

Backflow Preventers:

The water utility company is responsible for protecting the public water supply from any possibility of contamination. The utility company requires a backflow preventer (BFP) to prevent backflow or reintroduction of used or contaminated water in to the water supply lines. Backflow preventer prevents water inside the building from flowing back and mixing with city water.

Hot Water Delivery System:

Hot water is delivered to the end user fixture in one of three ways. First is through the use of a central boiler system. Second is the use of individual water heaters and third is with the use of an individual tankless heater.

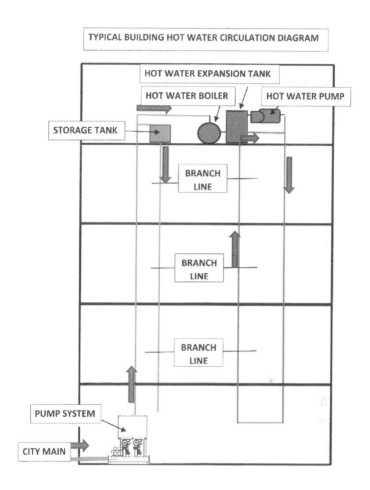

A boiler is an enclosed vessel in which water is heated or boiled and is then circulated from the boiler as hot water to the end user fixture. A hot water boiler consists of a fuel burner(s) that heats cold water traveling through coils inside the tank, an ignition source, a refractory liner that protects the surface on which the boiler is installed, a heat exchanger, a circulating pump and an expansion tank. In a hot water system, the water in the boiler is kept at approximately 180°F, but is brought down to 110°F before delivery to faucets. The burner cycles on and off to keep the water in the boiler at the right temperature, while the circulating pump cycles the water on a constant basis through the hot water loop to provide a consistent temperature of supply to the end user fixture.

Water heaters are common and are used frequently for residential dwelling hot water needs. They typically resemble large metal cylinders or drums that are often located in a separate enclosure within the dwelling. A water heater is basically a drum that is filled with water and equipped with internal dual heating elements on the top and the bottom of the tank or inside. The tank of the water heater is the inner shell of heavy metal containing a water protective liner that holds 40 to 60 gallons at any one time depending on the size of the heater installed based on the design needs. Water enters the water heater through the dip tube at the top of the tank and is then heated at the bottom. The shut-off valve located outside of the heater stops water flow into the water heater. The heat-out pipe allows the hot water to exit the water heater through the top of the tank. The drain valve allows for empting the heater and is located at the bottom of the tank. The dip tube feeds cold water from the water supply lines to the bottom of the tank. The heating mechanism stays on until the water reaches the preset temperature. As the water heats, it begins rise to the top of the tank. Water exiting the water heater at the top through the heat-out pipe is always the hottest in the tank at any given time due to the nature of hot water to rise above cold water which is denser. The second heater energizes when demand exceeds the capability of the lower element.

Tankless systems avoid loss of heat from water from being unused in the tank and only heat water that is coming in directly for use. The elimination of the tank makes this system more efficient. However, tankless water heaters are sized based on demand. The more fixtures operate at the same time the larger the unit requirements. Further, tankless water heaters require a larger electrical load compared to tank type water heaters.

A tankless water heater uses a powerful heat exchanger to raise the temperature of the incoming water supply. A heat exchanger is a device that transfers heat from one source to another. The heat exchanger in the case of the tankless water heater transfers heat generated by electric coils to the water that comes out of the faucet. This heat exchanger is activated by the incoming flow of water and heats the cold water to your preset temperature.

Drainage:

The drainage system of a multi-dwelling building divides in to three categories: waste water, storm water and condensate. Waste or sanitary water drainage system is defined as removal of used water from showers, toilets, dishwashers and other plumbing fixtures that are utilized for hygiene and house hold utility needs. Storm water drainage system consists of the removal of natural elements such as rain water from roof tops and decks as well as from other open areas that are at risk of flooding. Condensate drainage is a separate drainage line that is utilized for the removal of what is considered clean water from air handling units. This water may exit the building utilizing storm water lines.

In the waste or sanitary drainage system for a multi-story building, the drains from the plumbing fixtures are connected to vertical drain stacks that convey the waste and sewage to a point below the lowest floor of the building. For buildings 10 stories and higher, the drainage stacks require relief vent connections at specified intervals from the top, and connected to a vent stack that ends slightly above the roof. This relieves and equalizes pressure in the drainage stack to maintain the water seal in traps serving plumbing fixtures. Without allowing air to escape through the ventilation system in multi-story buildings kitchen sinks, for example, would simply not drain. The sanitary drainage system from a building usually discharges to the public sewer by gravity. However, when the lowest point of drain pipe connecting to the public sewer is lower than a public connection a lift station is utilized. A lift station collects waste water and pumps it to the level of the public sewer system for further discharge.

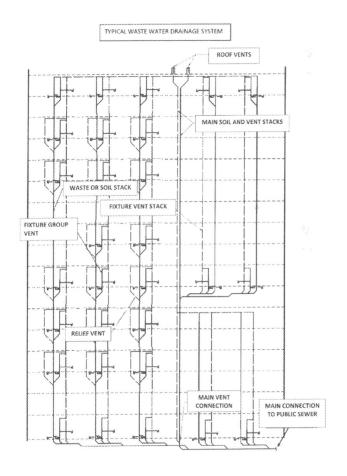

Storm water systems move rainwater from building roof top drains, area drains and subsoil (such as found in pool deck planters) drains to a point of discharge within the public storm water management system. Storm water drainage systems include only natural water and may not carry water there that has been contaminated by chemicals or waste. At times storm water is directed to the reuse water connection where it is delivered for treatment and returned for use in sprinkler systems.

Condensate drainage system is used in servicing air-conditioning system. Condensate drainage from air-conditioning equipment is extremely important, especially in humid environments where there is a lot of moisture in the air. When the air is cooled through an air-conditioning process, this water is condensed out of the air. All cooling coils in an air-conditioning system must have a drain pan under the cooling coil to collect the condensed water (condensate). A path is required to allow this condensed water to discharge to the drainage system without mixing with other drainage systems, besides storm drainage.

Trash Chute

The trash chute in a residential building may be considered one of the most vital but at the same time the most underappreciated components of the building. The trash chute is an efficiency mechanism that supports the quality of life and safety of its users. Regular maintenance and inspection is vital for seamless functionality of this vital component.

The trash chute system may be divided in to three parts; trash collection area, the trash chute riser and the roof top vent.

Trash Collection Area:

In most buildings, the trash collection area is a separate enclosure that houses the dumpsters (trash receptacle), trash compactor and the trash chute discharge door.

The dumpster is the end trash receptacle that is filled and then emptied by the garbage removal company. Frequency of the removal depends on occupancy with considerations made for seasonal fluctuation. Holydays and increased seasonal occupancy may warrant additional service visits. The dumpster container itself is typically provided by the garbage removal company which is also responsible for its replacements and repairs. Rust, broken wheels and separation on components must be reported to the vendor and arrangements made for resolution of problems.

The trash compactor is commonly used in mid and high density residential buildings as an efficiency components. The compactor is connected to the trash chute discharge door at the top and the receptacle at the front. The trash compactors consist of a motor-operated press head which compresses itself into the receptacle and returns itself back into place thereby permitting additional space.

The trash chute door discharge is the bottom opening of the trash chute riser. This component of the system is the first line of defense against fire initiated in the trash room to prevent flames and smoke from traveling up though the chute. This is achieved by the automatic door that must exist on all trash chutes. This simple but important device is commonly referred to as the "guillotine". In the event of a fire the fusible link that holds open the sliding spring operated door will melt at $F165^0$, thereby releasing the door shut. The guillotine is inspected on an annual basis by the fire department and must also be inspected by the in-house staff on a regular basis. Some municipalities now require that fusible links be replaced annually.

Trash Chute:

Trash chutes are tube sections stacked to whatever height is necessary to meet the needs of a residential structure. The standard metal trash chute may be made from stainless steel, galvanized steel or aluminum coated steel 16 gauge and heavier. The construction of the chute is such that the interior of the chute is completely free of any protrusions and the sections are joined in such a manner that water can flow directly through without escaping through the sides.

The trash chute should be cleaned on an annual basis. The cleaning is done by lowering a hose with a special nozzle that shoots pressurized, highly heated water on the circumference of the chute. This process removes any built-up grease from the interior of the chute. Removing the grease is important since it will act as an accelerant for fire, as well as removing any smells that may remain in the chute.

Trash Chute Doors:

Trash chute deposit doors are located on every occupied floor and are enclosed in rooms separating the trash chute door from the residential environment. Every trash chute door must be self-closing and self-latching and must not have any part protruding in the chute space. Trash chute doors must be inspected and maintained regularly for operational performance. Doors that do not close or latch properly creates a hazard that in the events of a fire will allow smoke to enter an occupied floor. The trash chute doors are fire resistant to 1.5 hours.

Most modern trash chute systems are built with fire sprinklers that are located above the trash chute door assembly inside the space between the actual chute riser and the door but not protruding in to the area through which materials travel down. These sprinklers are installed at alternating floors or at every other floor, with mandatory sprinklers and smoke detectors installed the end discharge which is the trash room.

Trash Chute Roof Top Vent:

The roof top vent is installed for the updraft within the trash chute to occur. As the hot air from inside of the building rises it removes odors form inside the chute. Additionally, the vent serves a fire protection objective by directing smoke up through the chute and allowing it to safely escape through the vent. Roof top vents are covered to protect from water intrusion that may lead to rust and have metal screen installed to prevent debris and small birds from entering the system.

The basic components of the trash chute system are the same throughout all residential buildings. However, add-ons to the system exist. Additional mechanical components that allow for recycling, automatic chute cleaners and roof top vent modifications are on the market. This life quality and safety system should not be overlooked, despite a humble aura it is an irreplaceable part of any residential building.

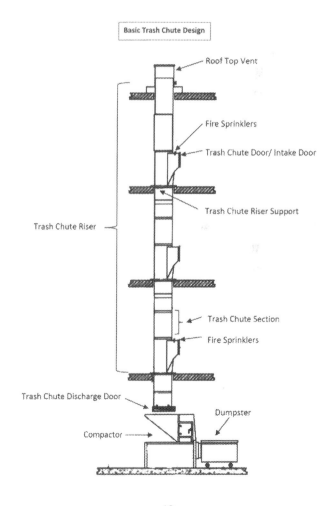

Basic Trash Chute Design

Roof Top Vent

Fire Sprinklers

Trash Chute Door/ Intake Door

Trash Chute Riser Support

Trash Chute Riser

Trash Chute Section

Fire Sprinklers

Trash Chute Discharge Door

Dumpster

Compactor

Building Electrical Supply

Building heating, cooling, lighting, function of mechanical components and appliances cannot operate without electricity. Electrical power is supplied to the various end user equipment by a serious of cables, wires and devices that manage the power of electrical supply for safety and efficiency.

Basic units of measurement that are used when discussing electricity are voltage (V), current (I, uppercase "i") and resistance (r). Voltage is measured in volts, current is measured in amps and finally resistance is measured in ohms.

To understand these electrical terms, one must look no further than the water pipes supplying water. The pressure in the pipes is represented by voltage (V), the rate of flow is equivalent to current (I) and the actual size of the pipe is the resistance (r). This analogy is helpful to understand the economics of supplying electricity to end-user device. However, to further understand the systems of electrical design in a residential structure attention must also be given to the means of management of electrical supply which are briefly described below.

An **electrical circuit** is a closed loop containing a source of electrical energy and a load such as a devise or equipment that needs to be powered. Conceivably all the electrical energy in a circuit must be used by the load. The load will convert the electrical energy to function, such as a running hair dryer. A circuit with no load is called an open circuit. In an open circuit, the power source feeds all its power through the wires or other conductive material to ground and back to itself. An open circuit that brings back unused energy may cause malfunction or damage.

Conductors are materials through which electrical current moves freely. A conductor is any component that allows an electrical charge to move through it. In contrast **insulators** are materials which prevent the flow of an electrical charge.

Switches control the flow of current through a junction in a circuit.

Relays are switching devices.

Thermistors change resistance in reaction to varying temperature.

Photoresistors change resistance in reaction to varying light.

Ground is the point in a circuit where the potential energy of the electrons is zero. At all times the ground is connected to a common point which is connected to the main service feeder. This provides for personal safety, equipment and building protection, as well as reducing electrical noise. It is important to note that terms such as bonding, earthing and even lighting protection are extensions of a grounding system, and can be further reviewed by referencing the National Electrical Code (NEC) Article 250.

In understanding the means of energy supply to power various components of a residential property it is best to follow the path of electricity through the building as further outlined.

Nearly all buildings are supplied power by the local utility company. Although alternative methods of energy supply exist they are few now and will not be discussed in this work. The local utility supplies the property with electricity either through an overhead connection but typically for newer buildings via the underground connection. The underground connection is enclosed in conduit which allows for easy access for maintenance and repair by the power provider such as Florida Power and Light.

The power supply connection accesses the building through what is called the service entrance into the electrical vault. Immediately before the entry, however, supply is measured by a kilowatt meter (the house meter) to determine consumption by the property. The house meter is always located upstream of the main disconnect so that it can never be turned off. Additionally, in multi-unit buildings banks of meters are installed to measure individual consumption by the occupants. Always remember, as designed current will always return to its voltage source.

A grounding rod is installed firmly into the earth to allow for dissipating discharge voltage to earth.

The electrical vault consists of transformers that step down high voltage supply allowing for service distribution. Transformers are used to step down incoming 4160-V supplied by the utility company to 480-V which is distributed throughout the building. Further, additional transformers are used to again step down 480-V to 120-V used for receptacle circuits. Voltage is divided in to two categories called "low" or "secondary voltage" with ranges of 120, 208, 240, 277, and 480-V. The second voltage category is "high" or "primary voltage" with ranges of 2400, 4160, 7200, 12,470, and 13,200-V which is used for industrial and power delivery needs. Within a residential building secondary voltage can also be divided in to two categories 120/240-V which may be considered household voltage. More specifically, 120-V is used to power most household devices such as televisions, toasters, computers and lamps and 240-V is used to power larger household components such as clothes dryers, air handlers stove ovens and compressors. The higher secondary voltage category of 277/480-V is used to power service components of the buildings. For example; 277-V is utilized in common area lighting and 480-V is used to power elevators and the HVAC system.

The electrical vault is a well-ventilated, fire rated room inside the building at times next to the switch gear room. However, to reduce costs, heat and ease maintenance by the power provider the transformer can be placed outside on a separate concrete pad.

The switch gear room contains first of all the main disconnect that controls power supply to the entire building with the exception of any emergency equipment, common lighting and elevators that are also powered by the emergency generator. In addition to the main disconnect there is additional service equipment such as secondary switches, fuses and circuit breaker panels that protect the end user equipment throughout the building.

The main switch board panel is located next to the main service connection and serves as a device to minimize voltage drops. The main switch board consists of switches, overcurrent and metering instruments for distributing and protecting a set number of electrical circuits as they connect to panel boards along with individual end user meters and individual main disconnects to the client service panels.

The purpose of the panel board which is typically located in the electrical closet to service large areas or is combined with switchboards to form individual service panels while servicing individual apartments or inside single family homes is to distribute, control and protect a number of branch circuits. The panel board hosts circuit breaker switches that interrupt the current or "trip" when experiencing an overload in current. This is a safety feature that protects the end used equipment from experiencing an overload in electrical supply that can lead to damage of fire.

The panel board is host to the wiring circuits or "branch circuits" that supply the power to end points of utilization, such as; lights, electrical outlets, AC, water heaters and other equipment requiring power. These circuits are divided in to "general" that supply electrical outlets for various uses and lighting. The design of these circuits depends on the number of outlets and types of devices serviced, "appliance" circuits supply power to appliances that need an individual circuit such as a refrigerator and a microwave oven that are usually in near proximity from each other and may be placed on the same circuit. "Individual" circuits are meant for supplying electricity to a single piece of equipment not only inside an individual dwelling but most commonly to those components servicing the common elements such as HVAC and exterior or lobby lighting. Circuits that supply outlets that are exposed to wet or humid condition such as those located outside, near pools or fountains or in the bathroom or kitchens must be protected by a "ground fault current interrupter" of "GFCI". The GFCI electrical wiring devices disconnect a circuit when it detects that the electrical current is not balanced between an energized conductor and the return neutral conductor. This imbalance is magnified by wet or damp environments and the circuit is opened to eliminate potential injury to personnel and/or damage to building equipment.

Safety must be top priority when dealing with electricity not only for in-house personnel but, also enforced with every vendor working at the property.

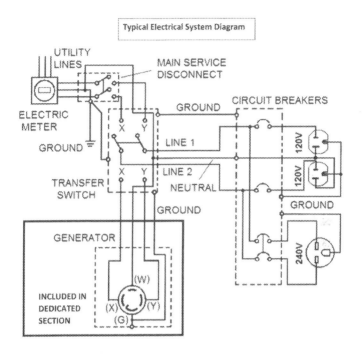

Standards for Electrical Safety Practices While Performing Maintenance:

1. Provide personal protective equipment and other protective equipment needed to protect employees from potential arc flash and shock hazards.

2. Provide training to create qualified employees capable of understanding the purpose and function of the electrical power supply and control equipment, as well as how to recognize and avoid the hazards associated with its operation and maintenance of equipment.

3. Treat all electrical conductors and circuit parts as though they are energized until they are placed in an electrically safe work condition with the following steps:

1. Identify the circuit or equipment to be de-energized and all possible sources of electrical energy supplies to the specific circuit or equipment.
2. Load currents must be interrupted appropriately before opening the circuit disconnecting device(s).
3. Verify, where safe to do so, that the appropriate circuit disconnecting device is indeed open.
4. Apply lockout/tag-out devices according to a documented and established procedure.
5. Test for absence of voltage with an approved voltmeter (where the voltmeter is tested on a known circuit voltage prior to and immediately following application).
6. Ground the phase conductors or circuit parts before touching them where the possibility of induced voltages or stored electrical energy exists.
7. Apply ground-connecting devices rated for the available fault duty where the conductors or circuit parts being de-energized could possible contact other expose energized conductors or circuit parts.

Emergency and Standby Generator

Emergency generator systems provide temporary power to vital components of a facility in case of a power outage. These systems are vital in the event of an emergency and although "out of sight", they may not be out of mind. Regular testing, in-house and professional maintenance must occur on a scheduled basis to keep these systems ready for an unpredictable emergency.

Generators Defined:

National Fire Protection Association defines two levels of emergency generators suitable for discussion in this work. Level 1 or "emergency generator" is described by being able to power for life safety systems in a building such as lighting, fire protection and ventilation systems aimed at allowing safe egress in case of an emergency. Level 2 or "standby generator" is described by a wider scope of power supply in addition to life safety systems to include components such as elevators, HVAC and hallway and lobby lighting.

A noteworthy difference between emergency and stand by power (generators) is that in addition to being an automatic system, emergency systems are separate distribution systems. They are installed as their own free standing supply with separate panels and Automatic Transfer Switch (ATS). The wiring for these systems must run separate raceways and placed in their own conduits.

Emergency generators are typically 200kW or less and are typically powered by gasoline, #2diesel or natural gas. Standby generators are much larger units than emergency generators and are powered by diesel due to the higher cost of gasoline and lack of availability to safely and efficiently provide large enough gas line to power these units. Standby generators can generate between 200kW and 2000kW (2MW) worth of electricity.

Both Emergency and standby generators are "engine driven". An engine driven generator consists of three basic parts. First it is the space housing the unit, which must provide a secure environment that is well ventilated and sound absorbent. The second part consists of the "gen-set" or engine and generator itself with the control panel and the exhaust accommodations. Lastly, the third part is the fuel storage including the fuel tank as part of the unit and additional fuel supply if applicable. Limited ability to store needed fuel inside the building creates a need to contract a fuel supply company which will deliver fuel to the site in the event of an emergency.

Typical Generator System:

Both emergency and standby generators are stationary pieces of equipment that are hard wired to the building's electrical system via an automatic transfer switch (ATS). An automatic transfer switch is much like a thermostat inside a home, but instead of monitoring temperature it monitors the utility power. The switch will automatically turn on the generator when it senses a loss in power. The automatic transfer switch will then transfer the load from the main power supply to the generator.

The vital nature of the standby or the emergency generator in combination with the unpredictable nature of its intended use warrants a very high emphasis on its maintenance. Poorly or improperly maintained generators are more likely to fail when needed most.

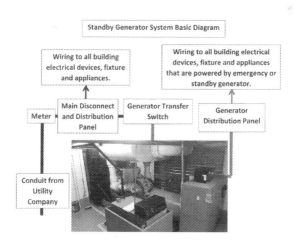

Typical Generator Maintenance Practice:

Utilizing regularly scheduled comprehensive generator maintenance and testing programs is the first step in assuring that the generator is operational and can be counted upon during an emergency. Contacting a licensed and insured contractor that specializes in emergency and standby generators is the first step in keeping the generator in proper working order. Quarterly inspections and maintenance by a qualified licensed contractor are ideal. All maintenance practices must be based on original manufacture's recommendations. A regular maintenance program will include checking fluid levels, changing lubrication oil, coolant, air filters, fuel servicing, and testing the starting system, including the batteries and charger. Additionally, regularly running the engine-generator will keep it performing at optimum levels.

Typical In-House Generator Maintenance Practice:

Weekly exercising of the gen-sets in new or updated models is programmed automatically at a predetermined time and day. In-house inspection should be performed on a weekly basis at a minimum. The housing for the generator must be kept clear of any debris to make sure that there is sufficient ventilation during operation of the unit. When the generator is not running, visual inspections of belts, wiring, radiator and engine block should be performed to make sure that they are not leaking and are in good operating condition. Exhaust system inspection should include the manifold, muffler, and exhaust pipe. All connecting welds, gaskets, joints and hangers must be checked for potential leaks and rust. Starter and electrical system terminals must be cleaned to keep it free from buildup of dirt, dust and oil residue. Connections must be checked for tightness and that they are free from corrosion. Any noted deficiencies must be corrected immediately by qualified personnel depending on the issue.

Records Keeping:

A record of all performed maintenance and inspections of fluid levels as well as test results will enable more accurate planning of future maintenance. Logs of recording maintenance and inspections are important for warranty and liability purposes and are to be well-maintained.

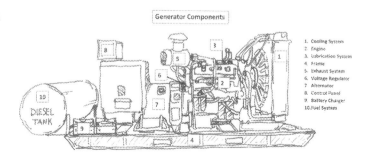

Generator Components

1. Cooling System
2. Engine
3. Lubrication System
4. Frame
5. Exhaust System
6. Voltage Regulator
7. Alternator
8. Control Panel
9. Battery Charger
10. Fuel System

HVAC

One of the most complicated mechanical components of any building is the HVAC system that provides the management of air and temperature throughout the conditioned ventilated spaces. HVAC systems are a combination of trades and sciences including thermal dynamics, fluid mechanics, electrical and mechanical engineering and refrigeration. However, it is important to have a basic understanding of the HVAC system design and components as well as the basics of their function.

The acronym HVAC stands for: Heating, Ventilating and Air-Conditioning and is comprised of a variety of electrical and mechanical components required for thermal management within a residential building.

The acronym's first letter, "H" as for heating, is a descriptive term for the system's function of adding heat to a space to maintain a desired temperature by counteracting the loss of heat to the external environment. The ventilating function described by the letter "V" is employed for moving a balanced percentage of fresh air or at times percentage of air into or out of a space to maintain a desired balance of CO_2 and oxygen and to help mitigate unwanted odors and enhance air quality within a conditioned space. The "AC", for air-conditioning refers to controlling the state of recirculated air which is temperature and humidity. An air-conditioning system function will lower or raise the temperature of the air dependent of the desired comfort level for the occupants. A correctly functioning system will do this and if it is designed correctly and functioning effectively, will control the desired percentage of humidity between 55% and 65%. The main problem that is relevant to conditioning a space, and is resolved with a HVAC system is how to provide the needed comfort factors in a space, and take the unwanted factors out of a space. The comfort factors such as; adding or removing humidity, adding or removing heat and moving the air to provide an even comfort level are performed by the HVAC system through a serous of related thermal cycles. These four basic cycles are: Supply Air and Return Air Cycle function is to provide a flow of supply and return air through the air conditioning equipment. The Chilled Water Cycle function is to provide chilled or hot or evaporating or condensing refrigerant to provide the medium to change the temperature of the air. Compressive Refrigeration Cycle function is to provide a refrigeration cycle to accomplish an exchange of heat. Heat Transfer Cycle function is to provide the means of heat transfer away from or to a conditioned space through equipment using water or air such as air cooled condensers, cooling towers or wells.

These four cycles are the basic operations and are found in all HVAC systems. These cycles can be provided by either system such as roof top packaged AC systems or split systems where two air handling functions are separate from the rest of the system. The management of the cycles is performed using a control system that calculates and directs the performance of individual mechanical components to meet the desired comfort settings.

Supply Air and Return Air Cycle:

This is the first cycle that begins in the actual conditioned space such as a hallway or a lobby. The first factor at play within the conditioned space is the dry and wet-bulb temperatures. The dry-bulb temperature is the measurement of heat percent in the space which is measured most often in Fahrenheit (^{0}F) or (^{0}C) in metric. The wet-bulb temperature is the measurement of humidity in the air or what is felt with moving air on wet skin.

The dynamic of conditioning a space is hinged upon removing undesirable conditions with opposing forces. This means that by providing colder and dryer air than the air that is currently there, the existing conditions will be circulated out by the new.

The supply fan is the piece of equipment that allows for the required air to be forced into the conditioned space and in addition, is the same fan that returns the undesired air back in to the cycle.

Once the undesired air re-enters the cycle, some of it is ejected as exhaust while remaining air is mixed with new outdoor air. The mixed outdoor and remaining air is passed through a filter and is managed back through the cooling and dehumidifying step which is performed by a cooling coil (heat exchanger). The cooling coil is lined with tubes and is packaged in between metal fins through which air is passed. Through the tubes of the cooling coil cold liquid is passes which absorbs the heat of the air thereby cooling it as it passes, in colder climates this function is reversed to supply heated and humidified air to the conditioned space with separate heating coil instead of cooling. In this example, the cooled air after passing through the cooling coil is passed through the variable-air-volume system which controls quantity of air supplied to the conditioned space by comparing set pints of the desired settings in the conditioned space. This control is done with the use of an airflow modulation device in the system that maintains the quantity of cold air and a terminal unit connected to the settings in the conditioned space of each zone. Zones are the individual conditioned spaces with varying desired conditioning levels such as hallways, offices or retail spaces. In smaller buildings or spaces the variable-air-volume system is interchanged with constant-volume system which only controls the quantity of air supplied with a basic on and off function.

The above described processes exist in all conditioning examples staring from window AC units that use these processes on a miniature scale to larger central air handler units that are commonly installed in separate rooms to condition spaces such as gyms and party rooms that may be too inefficient to link with the main supply air and return air cycle used to cover large spaces with similar conditioning needs.

The supply-air distribution system is essentially the corridor through which air travels. It is comprised of a duct system arranged in the overhead with vents as exit point in to the conditioned space.

Although the first cycle has been described to conclusion it is connected to the next cycle, the chilled water cycle that supplies the chilled liquid to the cooling coil (heat exchanger) that conditions the air.

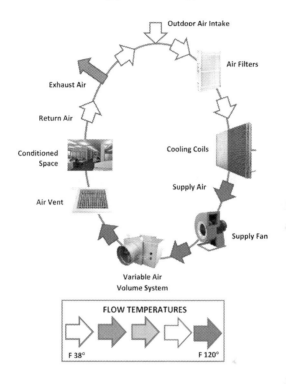

Supply Air and Return Air Cycle

Outdoor Air Intake

Air Filters

Exhaust Air

Return Air

Conditioned Space

Cooling Coils

Air Vent

Supply Air

Variable Air Volume System

Supply Fan

FLOW TEMPERATURES

F 38°   F 120°

Chilled Water Cycle:

In the chilled water cycle the cooling coil (heat exchanger) dehumidifies and removes heat from the air thereby cooling it as is passes through the coils. The process of cooling the air as it passes is achieved by removing the heat from it. The heat in the passing air is absorbed by the cooler temperature of the liquid passing through the coils in turn leaving the cooling coil at a warmer temperature having absorbed the heat from the air. Air, on the other hand leaves the cooling coil at a colder temperature than it entered. In effect the cooling coil had performed a heat exchange.

In order for the cooling coil to perform the heat exchange the liquid passing through its coils must be colder than the temperature of air for the exchange to occur. The cold liquid is supplied to the cooling coil by being first cooled by a piece of equipment called the evaporator. The evaporator resembles the composition of the cooling coil in the way that is also shell with tubes inside through which refrigerant is passed. As the liquid that had already absorbed the heat from the air as a function of the cooling coil (heat exchanger) enters and fills the evaporator shell the yet colder refrigerant passing through the tubes absorbs the heat of the passing liquid which leaves at a much colder temperature than it entered on its way back to the cooling coil.

The liquid is passed through the cycle from the cooling coil to the evaporator and back with a pump and the quantity of liquid cooled is controlled by the control valve. The control valve in the chilled water cycle acts to in response to the needs of the conditioned space in managing the quantity of the cooled liquid passed through the evaporator to the cooling coil since temperatures differ from the time of day and season respectively impacting the need for the quantity of cooling in correlation to the pre-set comfort levels of the space.

The chilled water cycle comes to an end when the cooled water from the evaporator reaches the cooling coil and starts heading back after the heat exchange had occurred. The evaporator is tied to the next cycle called the compressive refrigeration cycle which is key to providing colder refrigerant to the tubes of the evaporator for the heat exchange to occur.

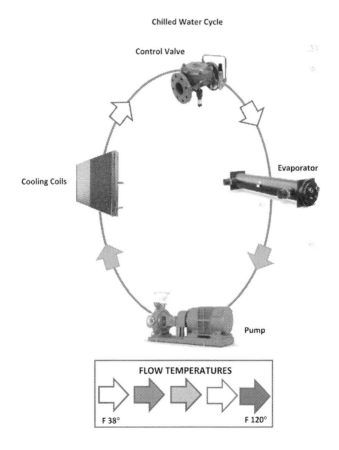

Chilled Water Cycle

Control Valve

Evaporator

Cooling Coils

Pump

FLOW TEMPERATURES

F 38°   F 120°

Compressive Refrigeration Cycle:

Compressive refrigeration cycle begins in the evaporator with the refrigerant that had absorbed the heat of the cooling liquid leaves the evaporator in a form of a vapor. This is much the same effect as if allowing a pot full of water to boil without stop; the liquid will turn in to a vapor.

Except in the dynamic of the compressive refrigeration cycle, the refrigerant vapor is passed to a compressor at low pressure where it is then compressed in to a high-pressure state which in turn further raises the vapor's temperature allowing it to move to the condenser.

The condenser is again an example of a heat exchange mechanism that allows the transfer of heat of the high temperature refrigerant vapor to a much colder absorbent liquid for example. When the bulk of the heat has transferred out of the refrigerant its temperature is dramatically reduced and it is back in its liquid state.

There are three main types of condenser units; air cooled, evaporative and water cooled. Air cooled units simply pass outside air over the tubes through which hot refrigerant vapor is flowing allowing the air to absorb the heat as it passes. An evaporative system works in the same way as air cooled except with water also being sprayed on the tubes through which hot refrigerant vapor is flowing assisting in the heat exchange. The air cooled and evaporative condenser units are installed outside on the roof or next to the structure in commercial settings and are a finalizing unit requiring no further cooling cycles after the completion of the compressive refrigeration cycle. A water-cooled system is comprised of a shell in to which the hot refrigerant vapor enters and a serious of tubes inside through which cold water is pumped. The cold water absorbs the heat decreasing its temperature and the vapor takes on a liquid state which is then drained and forwarded further through the cycle. A water-cooled condenser does need an additional cooling cycle, description of which follows further.

The cooled, but not cool enough liquid refrigerant is passed through at expansion valve. The expansion valve creates a very high drop in pressure and thereby dropping the temperature of the refrigerant. The drop in temperature makes the refrigerant cold enough to once more be cycled through the evaporator.

As the evaporator is the tie between chilled water cycle and compressive refrigeration cycle, the condenser (water cooled) is the tie between the compressive refrigeration cycle and the heat transfer cycle. As noted, the water-cooled condenser transfers the heat from the refrigerant to water. The heat transfer cycle cools the water so that the heat transfer can occur in the condenser once again.

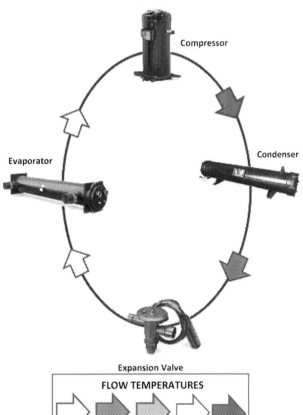

Compressive Refrigeration Cycle

Compressor

Condenser

Evaporator

Expansion Valve

FLOW TEMPERATURES

F 38°   F 120°

Heat Rejection Cycle:

In the heat rejection cycle water that had absorbed the heat of the refrigerant in the condenser is pumped in to a cooling tower where it is cooled. Cooling towers work by implementing evaporative cooling. This is a method of letting the water flow over the fill of the layers of the cooling tower along with air that is pulled down by rotating blades from the outside. The water is in turn cooled through evaporation and is again returned in to the cycle.

Because of the evaporation, cooling towers are equipped with floats which measure the level of water remaining for the cycle after evaporation. When the water quantity has decreased to an unsustainable level, additional water called the "make-up water" is added. High efficiency cooling towers are also equipped with variable drives that regulate the fans in correlation with outside temperatures, thereby conserving energy.

The now cooled water is circulated through the heat rejection cycle by a pump and the quantity of the delivery to the cooling tower is regulated by a control valve. The control valve manages the quantity of water to be cooled based on the cooling needs as it related to the external temperature which is colder at night and warmer in the day.

The heat rejection cycle is the last cycle that involves physical heating or cooling in the system. The next component of the HVAC design is the control system.

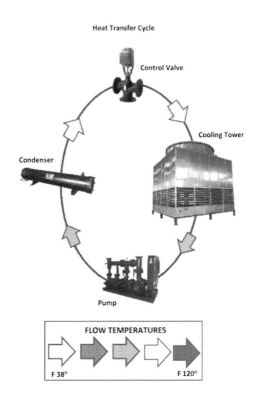

Control System:

The control system of the HVAC is first comprised of individual controllers for specific devices such as the valves, pumps, compressor, supply air fans and cooling tower. These equipment specific devices are connected to a central controller that supplies information for operations or the individual devices in correlation with the set points of desired levels. The complexity level of the controls varies from building to building, starting from the most straight forward to those involving computerized systems that monitor, diagnose and manage the system. These control functions may tie it to what is called Building Automation System that allows for management of other building components. But, however complex or basic the controls are the main objective of any HVAC system is to maintain comfort within a space.

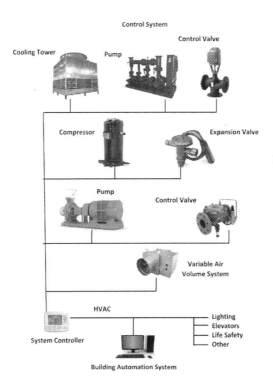

Fire Sprinklers

Fire sprinkler systems have become a standard requirement for large multifamily projects and in most scenarios, are required by Building Code and/or municipal ordinance. The fire sprinkler system is a vital life safety component of any building as well as a mitigating device in property loss.

Sprinkler systems deliver water to the site of increased temperatures resulting from instances of fire. Continuous improvements within the industry have dramatically reduced the instances of human error and malfunction of sprinkler systems creating them to be very reliable as a life safety component.

There are four main designs used for fire sprinkler systems. Wet-pipe systems contain pressurized water in the piping all the way up to the discharge location (nozzle). Dry-pipe systems contain pressurized air in the piping from the discharge location down to the valve next to the pump and are most common in geographical areas where pipes may be exposed to freezing temperatures. Pre-activation systems are a form of dry-pipe design with an additional operating feature of a controlling censor installed near the valve that is more sensitive to the conditions than the sprinkler head. These systems are installed to limit instances of accidental discharge and prevent damage to valuable materials. Deluge systems are systems that are open always and are activated to pump water into a space by a sensor device that detects heat, smoke or flames.

The wet-pipe system is most common for dense residential construction in Southeastern United States. Their composition mainly consists of a pump, piping, valves and sprinkler heads.

Fire Sprinkler Heads:

Aside from the open sprinkler heads used in the deluge system all other sprinkler heads involve a "head activation element" consisting of either material piece that either melts or most common have liquid that expands and breaks through its glass container at predetermined temperatures thereby releasing the water flow much like having the cork removed from a champagne bottle. The head activation elements are color coded to designate their heat tolerance rating.

Temperature Range (F)	Head Activation Glass Element Color
135-170	Red or Orange
175-225	Green of Yellow
250-300	Blue
325-375	Purple
400 and above	Black

The sprinkler heads exist in 3 main categories that relate to their installation. The Upright Head is installed in open areas without finish ceiling assembly on top of the branch pipe. The Pendant Head is use to be installed on the bottom of the branch pipe so it hangs down through the drop ceiling or is flush with ceiling utilizing ceiling caps. The Sidewall Head is installed at the side or tip of the branch pipe in a horizontal position off finished wall.

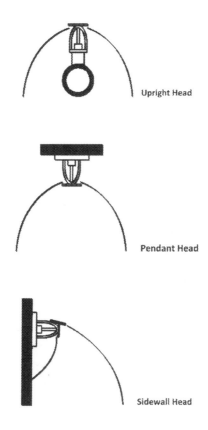

Upright Head

Pendant Head

Sidewall Head

Piping:

Water is supplied to the sprinkler heads through piping. Starting from the sprinkler head piping that carries water is called branch lines. Branch lines are configured in the design to provide optimal coverage to the areas that need to be protected. Branch lines are connected to the cross main lines which are distribution pipes that act as the middle man between the riser pipe and the end user branch lines with sprinkler heads. The riser pipes are the vertical water supply lines that deliver the water up to the cross main lines to be distributed. The riser lines are connected to the fire pump or pumps that pump the water up automatically when a drop in pressure is in the system is detected below a preset point. Interconnecting the piping system are valves that regulate the flow of water and enable for sections to be shut off. All shut off valves must be clearly designated as to their purpose for clarity in the event of emergency or maintenance processes. Sprinkler system piping is designated by red paint and must be maintained as such in all locations where visible with the exclusion of CPVC piping that is designated by orange and is supplied this way by the manufacturer. CPVC piping is installed downstream an acts as branch piping. Generally, these lines are concealed above ceilings and when repairs are necessary requires a Fire Watch. The connections of these lines are glued and require 24 hours to set before the branch can be pressurized.

Fire Sprinkler Pumps:

Pump assist systems are needed when local municipal water providers cannot meet water pressure to accommodate required standards. Fire pump is used to pump water through the fire sprinklers system. Most fire pumps installed are electrically powered, however diesel fueled pumps may also be found. The pump automatically engages after the jockey pump cannot maintain pressure caused by the flow of water out of the sprinkler head in the event of heat melting the head activation element. A jockey pump is an inline pump connected to the main fire pump. Jockey pump will maintain high set pressure. Jockey pump activity should be closely monitored by in-house personnel. Excessive starts and stops indicate seepage within the system. Activation of a single fire head will cause a drop in pressure that the jockey pump can no longer maintain. This drop will be sensed by the fire pump controller causing the pump to start. The activation of the pump triggers an alarm bell usually located near the fire pump room or the fire main line shut-off to alert of the activation. Safety codes and building standard dictate the size of pump needed for the fire sprinkler system to perform. Fire pump is connected to a secondary power source such as the emergency generator to be maintained in operation in case a loss of a power failure on the main line.

Water Supply:

Water supply is provided by way of city water main, but the main line is split in two branches, one providing domestic water to the building and the second devoted to fire protection needs. The supply of this line is operated by a stand-alone vale assembly which utilizes a fire backflow outside in the near proximity to the building next to the domestic water valve. The fire protection valve will always be painted red and must always remain open, except in the instances of maintenance. The valve will always indicate whether it is open. There are 2 types of valves which are screw and yoke control valve and the post indicating valve. In all instances the opened valve must be locked to prevent tempering due to the serious nature of its job.

An auxiliary means of supplying water in to the system is with the use of a Siamese pipe fitting. This fitting is installed on the lowest level of the exterior of the building and allows for pumping of water in the system by the fire department with the use of a pumper truck. This fitting consists of two or more connections allowing for uninterrupted pumping. Siamese fittings must be clearly marked and signage viewed from street as "F.D.C." Fire Department Connection.

Certification:

Certification requirements are set by local Fire Departments. Only a certified contractor with certified technicians may test and validate the system. Any problems with the system must be corrected prior to certification. Additionally, the fire backflow certification is separate from domestic water back flows and requires separate testing and certification.

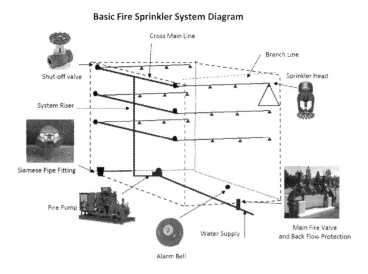

Basic Fire Sprinkler System Diagram

Elevators

As a manager of a building that utilizes an elevator system it is necessary to take steps to familiarize yourself with the equipment to promote safe and proper use. Regardless of the manufacturer, general elements of the elevator systems remain the same throughout. The purpose of this guide is to provide a basic overview of the functions and maintenance processes. Although certain maintenance methods are discussed, it is of outmost importance that regular maintenance and upkeep of the electrical and mechanical components of the system be performed by a certified elevator company employing certified elevator technicians.

There are two types of elevator systems; traction and hydraulic. Both traction and hydraulic refer to the means of ascend/descend of the elevator car. The basic descriptions of the two systems are included in the guide, as well as the homogenous components such as door assembly and elevator control systems are also included.

The final portion of the guide is focused on inspection and maintenance of the systems on their basic level as it would relate to the responsibility of the building management team and in cooperation with professional elevator maintenance contractors.

Traction Elevators:

Cables are used to suspend traction elevators. They are called traction elevators because the traction between the sheave or pulley and the cable enables the car to travel upwards and downwards because of the motion caused by the motor. For a very valid reason, the cables are termed as ropes. This is because initially, manila ropes were used in the installation of elevators. The modern steel cables have rope material in them to enable them to transfer lubricants to cables to reduce abrasion. The abrasion is caused when the cable continuously moves to and fro over the sheave (pulley). Modern traction elevator design involves between 4 and 8 cables per car with few exceptions. Every single cable can hold a completely loaded car. In case, all the cables fail, the car is suspended using the governor ropes. The governor ropes are connected to the car via a movable **actuator** device. When the governor **sheaves** locks upon freefall, the ropes actuate a system (like brakes) and brings car to a gradually stop. However, the risk of having even one cable break is very low due to the regular inspections commonly included in the maintenance contract. The cables are attached to the car on one end and to a group of counterweights on the other to balance out the load. Hoistway machinery is commonly installed on the roof, however they may also be installed in the basement and hoistways when permitted or required by design. Most traction machines have 1:1 roping configurations. This implies that the cable suspended over the pulley has the car on one end and the counterweights on the other. With every turn the sheave takes, the elevator will move a distance equal to the sheave's circumference. In case of a configuration of 2:1, the ropes go below the car while the elevator is hung on to a loop within the cables. Therefore, every time the sheave takes two turns, the elevator travels only the distance of a single turn. This minimizes the load burden on the motor and allows the use of smaller and faster motors.

Traction elevators can be either geared, which implies that they operate on gear system to transfer power to sheaves or they can be gearless, which means that they operate directly using the motor. As geared elevators have limitations regarding hoist way speeds, they are typically used in low or mid-rise structures. The device fitted inside a geared elevator comprises of a ring gear and a worm that decreases the speed of the motor and converts it into the power needed to raise the car. Smaller motors are employed in this kind of configuration to minimize the power and cost requirements. Faster speeds are required in high rise structures.

The basic components in a traction elevator:

- Motor (In the Machine Room)
- Main control device (Control Panel) that is used to:

  - Switch the motor on and off (In the Machine Room)
  - Control speed
  - Monitor weight capacity
  - Allow door to open/close
  - Gate guard components

- Device used to control the power supplied to an AC motor or equipment that produces DC power to a DC motor (In the Machine Room)
- Passenger or freight car
- Cables attached to a counterweight system
- Sensors that signal the controller

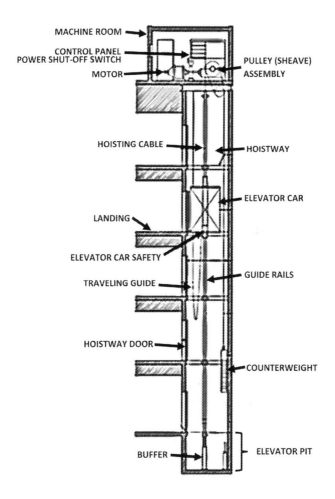

MACHINE ROOM

CONTROL PANEL
POWER SHUT-OFF SWITCH

MOTOR

PULLEY (SHEAVE)
ASSEMBLY

HOISTING CABLE

HOISTWAY

ELEVATOR CAR

LANDING

ELEVATOR CAR SAFETY

TRAVELING GUIDE

GUIDE RAILS

HOISTWAY DOOR

COUNTERWEIGHT

BUFFER

ELEVATOR PIT

Hydraulic Elevators:

These are the most common kind of elevators available.
Hydraulic elevators are the least expensive in terms of
installation and maintenance and are also inexpensive
to operate.

The easiest method of understanding the operational mechanism of a hydraulic elevator is to visualize an automotive repair shop that has lifts which can elevate the cars to allow the mechanic to do repairs. The hydraulic elevator is also a lift and has several basic components. The large silver tube rising out of the ground is called the hydraulic piston. Hydraulic fluid is pumped at high pressure inside the piston cylinder well that is buried beneath the ground. The piston elevates inside the cylinder to make space for the oil being pumped in. When the piston approaches its maximum stroke height, a locking device is activated to make sure that a decrease in oil pressure does not make the lift drop. To lower the lift or the elevator car, pressure is released by pumping the oil out of the piston cylinder well back in to the oil container.

The basic components of a hydraulic elevator:

- Hydraulic Piston
- Pump Assembly
- Controlling device
- Elevator Car

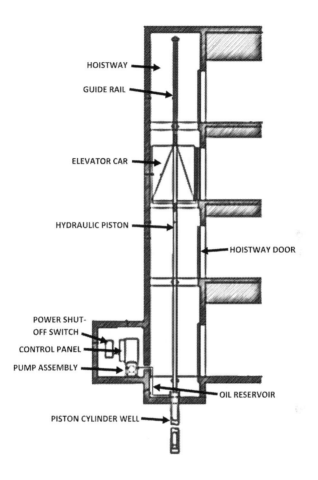

HOISTWAY

GUIDE RAIL

ELEVATOR CAR

HYDRAULIC PISTON

HOISTWAY DOOR

POWER SHUT-OFF SWITCH

CONTROL PANEL

PUMP ASSEMBLY

OIL RESERVOIR

PISTON CYLINDER WELL

There are two types of hydraulic elevator power designs; dry and submersible. In dry design, which includes a pump, motor and a valve that is mounted on the oil storage tank's exterior, mostly underneath. Dry power units need a larger quantity of oil and are air cooled. Dry power units are more expensive and use more space making submersible units a more cost-effective option.

In submersible power unit design the motor is mounted beneath the oil level inside the oil container. This gives the motor some cooling while the mounting of the valve and pump inside the tank saves ample amount of space. Not only do they save space, submersible units also consume less hydraulic oil. This reduces the effect of an oil spill in case the oil line gets ruptured and is also less expensive to fill.

Initially, hydraulic elevators that were built more than a century ago utilized water. That was substituted quickly by hydraulic oil which was and remains an industry staple. Regular hydraulic oil keeps its viscosity over a wide range of temperatures. Viscosity is essential in the way a hydraulic elevator levels at the landing and operates, for example; when the viscosity of the oil changes, the elevator's leveling characteristics will also change. The passenger car will stop too soon or too late making the car miss out on landing at the sill and can cause a tripping hazard.

The fluid movement in the system is managed by a main control valve. Most of the main control valves of today comprise of a minimum of four internal valves inside the housing that manage the hydraulic fluid distribution impacting the speed and ride quality of the elevator car. The valve system is guided by sensors positioned inside the hoistway. The sensors note the car locations and communicate with the control panel the needed factors to fulfill the cars destination objective.

Elevator Doors:

The door system is the most challenging component of an elevator. The doors need to open and close whenever the elevator moves. On average an elevator door opens and closes more than 200,000 times a year. This means that many components in the elevators move during this process and much wear occurs. In fact, doors are an integral part of the entire system since they are the only component that come in contact with the public continuously and can be a cause of injuries.

Also, there are doors that open in the center and have two single panels that move in opposite directions or 2, 3 and 4 panels on both sides that move in opposite directions. These are called two (three or four) speed center opening doors.

All passenger elevators have a motorized car door that moves with, and is a component of the elevator car. At every floor or landing, there exists a set of hoistway doors. These are just dead panels having no ability to open on their own. They may be loaded with springs to aid closing and to stay closed, however, they are mostly a sliding panel. These panels are basically suspended using an overhead track. Hoistway doors have rubberized wheels on the top that aid the door in rolling back and forth on this track. Doors that open in the center are attached by a cable. This implies that they are tied together using a cable and the doors are in the same position every time they move. These doors have devices known as gibs attached to the bottom. Gibs are nubs that protrude from the bottom of the door. They travel back and forth in a track set in the door sill at the bottom. They are used to hold the bottom door in its position and prevent it from swinging in or out. The door of the car is motorized and engaged to the hoistway doors with the help of a clutch assembly. This clutch protrudes a little to link with two small rubber rollers that jut out from the hoist way door. To fit inside the clutch, the rollers get compressed as the car comes down activating a mechanical apparatus that loosens the lock on the hoist way doors. These locks are attached to all elevators and are installed for safety in preventing the passengers from opening the doors.

The doors of most passenger elevators have a safety device fixed into them that retract the door from closing if it meets any form of resistance, such as a person or an object. The doors operate mechanically and must be regularly checked by a technician to ensure that they do not generate any force over thirty pounds before the motion of the door reverses. Any safety devices that are not adjusted properly may cause the assembly of the door to malfunction, resulting in potential injuries. Modern door safety devices are available with a set of electronic eyes. To retract the door, one needs to just break any one of the light beams. After a fixed time period, an alarm begins to sound and the door will gradually start to close. The closing force remains fixed at no more than thirty pounds in case someone may be lying incapacitated in the doorway.

For an elevator to operate properly, the doors of the car need to be completely closed along with all safety circuit contacts granting a closed loop. A set of contacts is attached to each set of hoist way doors and is fixed to the safety circuit. If the loop does not close because of something like wind related pressure in the building, a loosened spring, a corroded circuit contacts or for any other reason, the elevator will fail to operate.

In-House Maintenance:

The in-house maintenance which is performed by building staff is limited to cleaning and lighting. Although, these tasks are not difficult, they are very important to the safe operation of any elevator.

Machine Room: Machine room may not be used for storage. It must remain clean and have fully functional lighting at all times. Observe for any sign of water intrusion in to the room and repair immediately due to the large quantity of costly electrical equipment installed in the room.

Door Sills: Door sills on every landing and those of the elevator car must be free of dirt and debris at all time.

Inside Car: All interior surfaces must be cleaned in accordance with best practices be it wood or stainless steel. Lighting must be in full operation providing adequate illumination inside the car.

Emergency Phone: Emergency communication from the elevator car to another point of round the clock monitoring must be in full operation always.

Ride Quality: Attention must be paid to the quality of ride. Unusual sounds of continuous nature must be promptly reported to the maintenance service provider since they may be a sign of disrepair.

Inspecting the Elevator:

Inspections of elevator equipment are vital to maintain a good maintenance program. These inspections are performed with the professional maintenance provider with the attendance of building manager or chief engineer as they shadow the service technician. It is of upmost importance that a safe distance and all safety measures be observed when being near an elevator under inspection.

Key Inspection Elements:

All thorough inspections of elevator equipment must be done by a licensed professional and under no circumstance by in-house maintenance staff. The manipulation of the equipment is complicated and with many heavy, highly dangerous moving parts. All safety precaution, most of all a safe distance from equipment under inspection by a professional must be taken.

In the Car: Emergency communications, lights, noise, quality of ride, signal lights, cleanliness, condition of the overall interior and its fixtures, etc.

Machine Room: Cleanliness of the mechanical room. It is recommended to inquire about the role of every major component as well as what aspects are being checked by the technician.

In the Hoistway: The technician will inspect the door equipment; it is prudent to inquire from the technician about the status of its cleanliness. An estimate of 70% of elevator issues arises due to door problems. In case the door equipment is dusty and filthy, it shows that the elevators are not being properly serviced. The components cannot be checked to see if they are working properly if they are dirty and greasy. Further, in the case of traction elevators the cables are to be inspected as well as the various moving components and censors in the hoistway.

In the Elevator Pit: The pit must be inspected and cleaned by the technician. Even though dirty pits rarely affect the performance of an elevator, it indicates the conscientiousness of the service technician. The pit light must be in proper working order. Oil or trash on the pit floor is an indication that the technician is not attending to all the details and is not performing his job satisfactorily.

Top of Car: The top of car must be clean and rust free. The top light on the car should be in working order and the car top should not have any stored parts or trash on it.

General: Annual inspections will focus on the above-mentioned aspects as well as factors as related to Elevator Code Compliance as mandated by the State of Florida. Five year inspections which are referred to as the "Five Year Full Load" inspections are focused on the safety and operation of the elevator when operated at full capacity weight.

Elevator Emergency Operation:

Elevator emergency operation during an emergency is performed by emergency personnel. This includes the rescue of persons stuck in the elevator car and especially during situations involving fire and other events that are dangerous to the safety of the public and maintenance staff. However, being acquainted with the procedure is important.

Hydraulic Elevator Shut- off Switch:

The operational components of a hydraulic elevator system are found in the machine room. This is where the power cut-off switch to the electric motor and the hydraulic fluid shut-off valve that leads to the pump are located. If there are more than one elevator, all pumps and power shut-off switches are (must be) clearly designated with corresponding numbers.

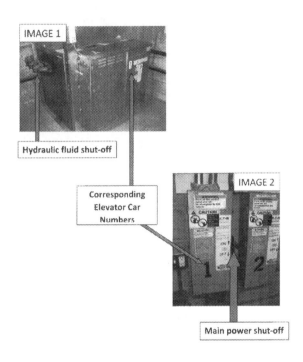

Emergency personnel (usually fire department) will assess the situation and depending on the circumstance may make the decision to shut off both the hydraulic fluid pump and the power to the pump. A circumstance that may call for this is retrieving passengers from a car that is stalled in between floors.

Traction Elevator Shut-off Switch:

Traction elevator electric motor and its power shut-off switch are found in the machine room. If there is more than one elevator in the same machine room, each motor numbered and a corresponding shut-off switch will be in close proximity.

IMAGE 3

Elevator Fire Department Recall Key:

The elevator key is used for emergency control of the elevator which overrides any and all calls or destinations for the car. The key is found in what is called a Knox Box which is placed in the main lobby next to the elevators and appears as a small metal box intended for quick access for the fire department.

There are three operations that are controlled by the use of the elevator key.

PHASE NORMAL

This is the status of the elevator when used by the public.

PHASE I

This function is often automatic. It brings the elevator(s) to a pre-determined lower level, or what is called a recall floor when the buildings alarm system has been activated. Phase I is also achieved by inserting an elevator key into the Phase I switch that's found in the lobby of the recall floor, usually the lobby. In most cases the recall floor is the first-floor lobby.

Elevators installed after 2005 will have RESET label instead of BYPASS labeled on the panel, however the function remains the same.

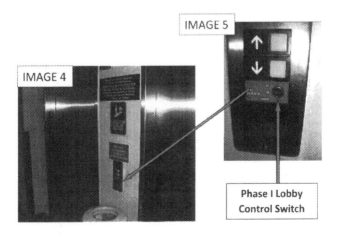

IMAGE 5

IMAGE 4

Phase I Lobby Control Switch

PHASE II

The operation of an elevator car in Phase II is performed from inside the car. In this phase, the elevator key is used to turn the Phase II key switch that's located inside the elevator, on the control panel.

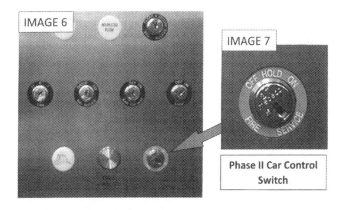

Phase II Car Control Switch

OFF – Normal operation. The Phase I key switch in the elevator lobby and the car's Phase II control panel switch should be in this position when restoring the system for normal operations.

ON – Before Phase II car control can be achieved, the Phase I lobby control switch mentioned above must be in the ON position. (Refer to images 5 and 7). Destination floor is to be selected. The elevator door will now only open or close by continuous pressure on the "Door Open/Door Close" button. When opening a door and if the button is released prior to the door reaching the fully open position, the door will close. This is also referred to as the "peek-a-boo" function. The "peek-a-boo" function allows for just a quick "peek" for the firefighter into the floor landing lobby. By pressing down the Door Open button the doors will respond by opening as long as the button is pressed, if released (in case of danger on the landing), the doors will immediately shut.

HOLD – Once arrived at the intended floor and the door is opened, switch the car control panel switch to hold. (Refer to image 7). The car will now remain at the floor with its door held open and the door close button will not function. The key can be removed to prevent someone from inadvertently taking the car.

BYPASS/RESET – When restoring the elevator system to NORMAL OPERATION and once the alarm system has been reset, turn the Phase II car control switch to OFF and return to the recall floor. Then turn the Phase I lobby key switch to BYPASS/RESET, then to OFF position. The elevator system is now ready for public use. Normal elevator function **cannot** be restored until this reset process is complete and all switches are in the OFF position.

The BYPASS function can also be used to give the fire department the use of the elevator(s) in normal operation while the alarm system is in alarm status. If the fire department has Phase II control of an elevator car, and the alarm system has been reset, the fire department may still require to control that car while returning all others in that bank to normal operation for public use. This can be achieved by simply turning the Phase I switch to BYPASS/RESET, then to OFF. Only that one car will now have Phase II firefighter control.

FIRE HELMET LIGHT – Most modern panels are equipped with this light. It **flashes** when a smoke detector in the elevator machine room has been activated. (Refer to image 8).

CANCEL – Pressing and releasing this button switch, the floor selection switch is cancelled and the elevator car is stopped at the next floor until another function switch is pressed. (Refer to image 8).

Although many lobby and car control switches have a different esthetical look, the function remains the same.

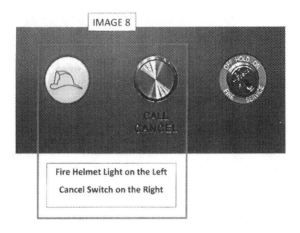

IMAGE 8

Fire Helmet Light on the Left
Cancel Switch on the Right

Elevator Technology:

Modern technological advents have had a dramatic impact on the elevator systems maintenance, operation and security. From common cameras inside the car and key card reader devices for added security to Elevator Control Desk (ECD) that allow front desk personal to track and manage the assent and decent of a car security and safety systems innovations are still improving and evolving. A higher accuracy of computerized diagnostics for elevator maintenance are being achieved with regularity and even the standard traction cable systems are gradually being replaced by belts that allow for faster speeds and higher elevator reaches. Alongside the progress that is continuously achieved and new standards recorded it is important to follow the developments within the elevator industry.

Building Envelope

A building envelope is the boundary between the interior and exterior of a structure. Typical components are walls, floors, ceilings, windows doors or any other components that act as the skin of a building. This system involving all the envelope components separate the conditioned spaces of the interior from the unconditioned exterior. The building envelope is made up of the foundation, windows, doors, walls and roof. Any decorative components are not a part of the building envelope system apart from paint which has a decorative aspect to it, but serves a vital functional purpose. However, decorative components that are affixed to the envelope must also be maintained since they can serve as conduit of exposure for structural elements, such as, water accumulating behind a decorative feature and impacting a masonry wall.

There are five fundamental functions of the building envelope. First is the structural support of the building; such as sheer walls. The second function of the building envelope system is to control the moisture factors that may impact the interior spaces. The most obvious of these components is the roof system that protects the building from harmful impact of rain and snow as a basic function. The third function is the control of the temperature and humidity of the conditioned interior spaces. This results by way of sealing in the functions of the HVAC system within the confines of the conditioned spaces. The fourth function is the control of the air pressure changes that my impact the conditioned interior spaces. This function is fulfilled by doors and windows with their various uses and designs ranging from balcony sliding glass doors to emergency exits to the outside. Finally, the finishing of the building envelope provides for visual appeal of the building impacting its value and desirability in the market place.

A "tight" building envelope describes the condition of the building envelope with few air leaks. A tight envelope allows for great control over energy efficiency and reduction of wear and deterioration within the condition spaces. A tight building envelope will also prevent the intrusion of water into the conditioned spaces minimizing the potential for mold and mildew.

On the other hand, a "loose" envelope construction may define a poorly constructed envelope that allows moisture in and air to escape negatively impacting the conditioned spaces. This can also be a result of poor maintenance practice. A loose envelope may also be intended in design, in instances where natural ventilation is most cost effective. An example of an intentionally loose envelope design is in a multi vehicle parking garage. In this instance, natural forms of air circulation is the most efficient way to protect the public from the harmful effects of the automotive exhaust.

Roofing:

Most common in high-density residential construction is the flat roof. These roofs are most economical to design, construct and maintain. Additionally, flat roofs allow for ease of access to other building components that may be located on the roof such a cooling tower or a traction elevator machine room.

Built-Up Roof

The built-up roof or BUR is the most common of flat roof systems. Its installation consists of applying three or more layers of waterproof material staggered with hot tar. The tar is then covered by a layer of aggregate which acts as a ballast, temperature control and fire protection for the assembly. The benefit to the built-up roof is economical. It is the cheapest roof to install and maintain. The negative factors of the built-up roof are that leaks or breaches within the system are hard to find as well and the messy environment this system created during installation. Additionally, gravel can become loose over time creating maintenance difficulties.

Modified Bitumen

Modified bitumen systems are oil base products that are applied by unrolling the membrane on to the roof surface. The membrane is secured to the roof with the application of heat during the unrolling process. This system has a higher degree of hazard during the installation due to the use of open flames. The price point characteristic of this system is in the middle range. This system is not as resistant to scuffing as the rubber membrane or the BUR systems so additional caution must be taken when working on the membrane surface. However, new peel-and-stick products are available on the market which removes the need for heat and decreases hazard.

Rubber Membrane

A rubber membrane roofing system is made from Ethylene Propylene Diene Monomer or EPDM and is a true rubber. This system is easily installed by mechanical means and is engineered to be highly resistant to scuffing, tears and sunlight. This roofing system is easy to repair if punctured but is the most expensive system of the three described.

Substrates:

The roofing system substrates or the base on to which an overlayment of Built-Up, Modified Bitumen or Rubber Membrane system is installed. The substrates are initially designed to for the particular type of construction and use of the roof. The substrates will have specific acceptable conditions for repairs and maintenance which must be provided by a certified roofing contractor or an engineer before engaging in repairs or establishing a maintenance program.

The substrates divide into 3 categories: metal, wood and concrete.

Metal substrates consist of a metal tray installed over the building's topmost elevation. The tray is then overlayed by perlite concrete (a light weight concrete material) to serve as an insulating layer.

Wood substrates are generally constructed from well-seasoned lumber of a minimum 1 inch thickness. Plywood is also used in substrates construction as well as structural wood-fiber. However, wooden and metal substrate systems are mostly utilized in construction of structures under 5 stories high.

Concrete substrates are mainly found in two forms. Cast in place decks are installed on sight by forming and pouring concrete to generate a substrate roof deck. Precast substrate roof decks are cast off site and are craned on to the necessary elevation.

Roof Maintenance:

Roof system can deteriorate from several factors ranging from normal wear and weather conditions to poor maintenance practices, as well as improper design or installation. Issues that are noted on the surface of the roof must be dealt with speedily or have the potential to degrade rapidly due to the high impact nature of the roofing system.

The main focus of maintenance as it serves management and engineering staff of a high density residential structure is inspection, reporting and records keeping.

When inspecting the roof, it must be determined if the roof system is performing according to its intended function. Signs of weakness, deterioration and hazardous condition must be identified. Finally, a determination must be made if repairs are needed.

In most circumstances roof repairs are performed by a licensed roofing company and it is a worthwhile engagement to maintain a service and inspection agreement with a licensed roofing company as well. However, inspection must be a regular task of the maintenance or engineering department.

In approaching regular roof inspections on the exterior, the focus must be kept on integrity and continuity of roof covering (overlayment). Inspection must also be performed on gutters, vents and exhausts that may exist on the roof as well as on any chemcurbs (protective buffer at the base which acts as a transition between equipment and roof) around support material that is used to secure equipment to the roof.

Where possible, inspections should be made on the interior, with focus on the finishes such as ceilings, walls and walls immediately below the roofing system. These inspections are focused on water infiltration and signs of structural defects.

All records of findings, maintenance and repair efforts must be kept for future reference. Also, record must be kept of locations with growing and potential problems. Photographing potential problem areas that may not yet be in need of repair will give one a better idea in time as to the extent of deterioration. Further, thermal imaging may also provide a clearer view of problems such as faults in the membrane's integrity. It is a good rule of thumb to inspect the roof after inclement weather in addition to annual and at least bimonthly inspection.

Exterior Walls:

Exterior walls of a building serve the function of separating the interior spaces from the external condition such as rain, wind, snow, sound, humidity and so forth. The exterior walls have many means of construction from timber or brick which are found in old style construction for single family dwellings to modern multi-unit buildings utilizing precast concrete walls to intricate poured concrete designs.

The focus of this section will be on the basic principles of wall systems as they appear in high-rise residential buildings and means of their maintenance.

The modern wall systems most importantly consist to weight bearing vertical columns that support the loads of floor slabs and roofing. The weight bearing columns and walls are engineered throughout the structure to efficiently support it and are coordinated with considerations of the intended interior design of the spaces. Shear walls which are also weight bearing are rigid vertical walls that are designed to carry horizontal loads such as wind and seismic impacts to the buildings foundation where it is absorbed.

The spaces remaining in between weight bearing walls are filled according to the architectural design. In most cases, it is a combination of cinderblock and window systems that create the majority of the buildings vertical envelope. Both concrete and cinderblock which is used to construct these vertical surfaces are porous materials and must be maintenance on a regular basis to prevent spalling, cracking and erosion.

Building Envelope Waterproofing:

Water penetration of the building envelope can lead to the deterioration of the various physical elements of the building. The impact may cause esthetic and most importantly structural degradation such as spelling of concrete which is caused by moisture effecting steel components of the structure making them rust and thereby expand to displace sections of concrete.

To understand the means of waterproofing a building it is important to first understand how water penetrates. First, water has to be present to impact the structure. Most common are natural causes such as rain and accumulation of ground water at the exterior of the structure. Second factor to understand in causes of water penetration is the existence of an opening through which water can pass. Such an opening can be visible and not visible to the naked eye. For example, the porous surface of concrete. Finally, a physical force must be present to move the water through the opening.

The understanding of the force involved can guide one to find the opening through which the water is intruding and mitigate it.

Gravity is the most obvious force that pushes water through an opening. Cavities in horizontal surfaces as well as damaged expansion joints will serve as a corridor for downward flowing water.

Passageway between exterior building materials can create suction causing the water to intrude. The smaller the passageway the greater the suction, to the extent that this suction can even make the water travel upward. This is most common in instance of water intruding through the top portion of window frames in between the glass and the frame.

Wind driven rain is caused by the wind currents and gusts that drive the rain on the vertical surfaces of the structure as well as in to crevices that might not be affected by rain without wind. Wind driven rain mostly impacts the corners and the top of the structure by creating a swirling pattern at these locations. The most impacted section of the structure due to this occurrence is the parapet walls.

Water can also intrude by tension. The physicality of the surface tension of water allows it to follow the vertical path down and then grab on to the horizontal path to intrude in to the interior space. This is most visible in instances of water intrusion at the space between the concrete structure of a window and the window frame at its upper most horizontal location.

The momentum with which rain is driven must also be considered. Wind driven rain may be pushed through a variety of configurations of building components. Most common example is the intrusion through the balcony sliding glass door assembly. There, the momentum of the water drives it around the corners and angles of the assembly to emerge in the interior space.

Pressure in rain fall scenario can lead to various behaviors of rain water resulting in intrusion of it in to the interior space. However, passive examples also play a factor in water intrusion. The chief example of which is called hydrostatic pressure which is most evident in ground standing water. Its abundance over time will impact the water proofing membranes of structural components underground. This will also impact exterior planters found on pool decks. Without proper drainage, water remaining in the planted will damage the waterproofing membrane inside the panted and will seep through to the exterior wall.

Prevention of water penetration:

It is impossible to prevent the forces of nature that deliver and force water on to structures. However, it is possible to mitigate if not prevent water intrusion with regular maintenance and inspections of possible weak areas.

Limiting water intrusion in to the air-conditioned spaces is best started at the roof. Inspection of these areas should focus on the continuation of the water proofing membrane of the roof in whatever system it exists. The concept of continuous system is highlighted by strength of seams and non-existence of tears. Additionally, close attention must be paid to joint locations and how properly detailed the flashing material is around the perimeter of the roof. Large openings such as expansion joints which are filled with elastomeric material must be monitored for locations with tears and dislodging. After repair, these locations must result in adherence to the concrete surfaces and be installed in a neat manner.

Waterproofing or commonly referred to as "painting" of the exterior stucco surfaces and sealing of internal transitions are an integral part of preventing water penetration. Stucco and concrete are porous and allow for moisture to penetrate, leading to such adverse effects as spalling or general deterioration of the concrete surface. Although there are a lot of products on the market that can be used, it is best to have a paint manufacturing company first compose a specification for the painting project that will be used. These specifications from a desired manufacturer will then be used by contractors to bid on the project, this is true for any surface that needs to be painted; including concrete, stucco and metals. The specifications will include the means of preparing the surface and repairing it if needed, the product to be used for the various aspects of the job and the means to apply them both in method and quantity to achieve the desired warranty from the manufacturer and effect.

The most common and regular approach to preventing water penetration is building masonry painting projects. These projects tend also to be the most expensive regular maintenance initiatives in most high density residential buildings.

As mentioned earlier, there are many products on the market that may be recommended for a painting/waterproofing project and the consideration of these products will occur during the initial meetings with the paint manufacturers' representatives and a certified engineer to compose the project specifications.

The cornerstone of building painting projects is elastomeric coating which has become the most typical product of choice and has retained its popularity for many years. Elastomeric coatings are currently being phased out by High-Build coatings which will be addressed next. Elastomeric paint was initially designed as waterproofing product for stucco, concrete and masonry walls. It is applied as a film due to its higher ratio of solids to water (or solvents) than conventional paint products. Some of the attractive qualities of elastomeric paint include film-like action, durability, and ability to stretch with natural movements of the structure as well as to bridge the gaps of hairline cracks of the concrete or stucco surfaces.

High-build coatings which have now gained great popularity have become so for a reason. These coatings are preferred for qualities, such as; resistance to wind-driven rain, high elongation and elongation recovery, ability to bridge cracks and water vapor permeability that allows any water that find its way behind the coating to seep out through the coating.

Just as in elastomeric coatings, high build paints are generally applied in one or two coats of 10-15 mils, in contrast to regular paint which is applied to 3-5mils. This dramatic difference in thickness is a result of higher content of solids contained in these products. High-build coatings contain approximately 50% solids in the product in contrast to regular paint which contain approximately 30% of solids. In high-build paints, solids are resins and fillers, a balanced combination of which determined the coating's properties. For example, additional sand or aggregate used in the coating can generate a variety of desire textures and a high amount of resin provides for an excellent protective film against rain.

To attain the aforementioned effects as well as the desired warranty period that can range from 8 to 10 years or longer, it is most important to monitor the preparation of the surfaces and the application of the product. These guidelines are found in the manufacturer's specification and in many cases inspected by the manufacturer's representative during the performance of the projects.

The surface must be diligently pressure cleaned to remove dirt, debris and loose paint from the surface. The painting specifications will give guidelines even for the pressure needed to clean the surface. Further the specifications will note if a conditioner or a sealer which is commonly referred to as a primer is needed. A primer improves paint's adhesion to the surface, provides additional protection to the surface and improves the durability of the paint. Finally, close attention must be paid to the application of both the primer (if needed) and the actual paint product. The number of gallons purchased must meet the amount of square feet to be painted. This is needed to be sure that the paint has not been thinned to conflict with specifications from the manufacturer which would void the warranty.

Prevention of Water Accumulation:

Accumulating and standing water cause deterioration of materials in contact with the water. Even pools of water that accumulate for only several days at a time after a rain will over time cause damage. To ensure that water does not accumulate on horizontal surfaces proper drainage must be maintained. First, drainage must exist or be installed where water has the potential to accumulate. Maintaining drainage mainly involves making sure that there is no obstruction preventing water from either entering the drain or flowing through it. Snaking the drain or jetting it at least annually will allow the drain to remain unobstructed and functional.

Windows and Doors:

In most modern high-density buildings, especially along coastal areas like Florida the most common window system is referred to as impact windows. These window systems are designed and engineered to withstand hurricane force winds and impact from debris. In buildings where windows do not meet impact window ratings, insurance incentives exist to make the change or to install additional protection such as shutters.

Window and sliding door systems in a high-density residential building play a pivotal role in maintain the pressure levels, humidity and air quality inside the dwelling and those of adjacent common elements.

Although rarely is it the responsibility of the Association of a building to maintain the windows and sliding glass doors of individual dwellings it is still of value to know the maintainable components of the assembly which are the rollers, tracks and locks.

A sliding balcony glass door utilizes rolled on the bottom of the frame which allow the window to slide open and closed. Over time these rollers become worn or collapse making the sliding of the glass door to either be hard or impossible all together. The rollers will need to be replaced.

The track or the aluminum rib may also become damaged by worn rollers. This will result in the sliding glass door to skip and feel uneven when being opened. The track will need to be repaired.

Finally, locks of the sliding glass door and windows need to be in operable condition in order for the window to perform its impact resistant function. If a lock is inoperable the openings will be compromised and fail not only in the sense of security but may be forced open by wind.

Exterior Doors:

A door has several passive operations; security, isolation from external elements such as weather or maintaining a conditioned environment and fire protection. Security aspect of a door hinges on the operating components such as locks, hinges, handles and door closers. These components need attention when wear and tear is noticed. Not resolving maintenance issues pertaining to a door will not only jeopardize its function of security but also impact life safety and conditioning aspects of its function.

The life and safety aspect of a door directly relates to its fire rating. A fire rating is the amount of time a door can withstand the heat of a fire before failing. Doors are rated based on the rating of the wall into which the door is installed, its location within the building and the prevailing building codes. Doors are rated 3/4 of the rating of the surrounding walls. To give an example; an envelope wall that is rated 4 hours may have a door that is rated for 3 hours. This calculation applies to all ratings except for those doors that are rated for 1/3 hour or 20 minutes which may be used on a 1 hour rated wall. However, a higher fire rating of a door than that of a wall may be used. The concept of fire rating a door is directly impacted by its condition. Disrepair will lead to the door's premature failure in case of a fire.

The final function of a door is to maintain the conditioned spaces and protect them from the elements. Doors that do not close tightly or close slower than designed will allow conditioned air to escape and external elements to enter. Properly operating door systems reduce energy consumption and prevent deterioration of internal elements.

Understanding the components of the building envelope is imperative to maintaining its functionality. Defects in any of these components will lead to deterioration of the conditioned spaces. Additionally, the deterioration may in many cases be less then observable such as in the case of water damage which can perpetuate the growth of mold, mildew or rusting. Care of the envelope is just as important as care for one's own skin.

References

An Introduction to Building Mechanical Systems, Tom Dontigny, Authorhouse, 2006

Building Codes Illustrated: A Guide to Understanding the 2006 International Building Code, Francis Ching, Steven Winkel, Second Edition, John Wiley & Sons, Inc., 2007

Building Construction Illustrated, Francis Ching, Fourth Edition, John Wiley & Sons, Inc., 2008

Building Technology: Mechanical and Electrical Systems, Benjamin Stein, Second Edition, John Wiley & Sons, Inc., 1997

Designing Tall Buildings: Structure as Architecture, Mark Sarkisian, Routledge, 2012

Electrician's Pocket Manual, Rex Miller, Second Edition, McGraw-Hill, 2005

Facility Manager's Maintenance Handbook, Richard Payton, Bernard Lewis, Second Edition, McGraw Hill, 2007

Integrated M/E Design: Building Systems Engineering, Anil Ahuja, Chapman & Hall, 1997

Landscape Maintenance and Lawn Care Business, Tim Roncevich, Steven Primm, Upstart Business Consulting Group, 2011

Mechanical and Electrical Equipment for Buildings, Benjamin Stein, John Reynolds, Walter Grondzik, Alison Kwok, Tenth Edition, John Wiley & Sons, Inc., 2006

Mechanical and Electrical Systems in Architecture, Engineering and Construction, Joseph Wujek, Frank Dagostino, Fifth Edition, Pearson, 2009

Plumbing Systems: Analysis, Design and Construction, Tim Wentz, Prentice Hall, 1996

Plumbing Venting: Decoding Chapter 9 of the IPC, Bob Scott, International Building Code Council, 2014

Project Management in Construction, Sidney Levy, Fifth Edition, McGraw Hill, 2006

Structural Analysis and Design of Tall Buildings: Steel and Composite Construction, Bungale S. Taranath, CRC Press, 2012

Sustainable Landscape Management: Design, Construction, and Maintenance, Ann Marie

VanDerZanden, Thomas W. Cook, John Wiley & Sons, Inc., 2010

The Green Studio Handbook: Environmental Strategies for Schematic Design, Alison Kwok, Walter Grondzik, Architectural Press, 2007

The Building Environment: Active and Passive Control Systems, Vaughn Bradshaw, Third Edition, John Wiley & Sons, Inc., 2006

Index

C

Rated 54, 58, 125

raveling 21, 26, 27, 28

Refrigerant 65, 70, 71, 72, 73, 74, 75

Refrigeration 64, 65, 71, 72, 73

Relays 51

relief vent 42

repairs 17, 20, 21, 25, 27, 28, 29, 30, 46, 52, 81, 90, 95, 110, 111, 112, 113, 118

RESET 102, 104, 105

resins 121

resistance 18, 26, 50, 51, 94, 120

Responsibility iv, 85, 123

Rib 124

Ride Quality 92, 96

Riser 36, 45, 46, 48, 81

Rollers 94, 123, 124

Rot 13

rubber membrane 110, 111

rusting 126

S

Sand 19, 27, 121

screen 48

screw 83

Scuffing 110

seal coat 26, 27

Sealer 121

Seams 118

Season 3, 8, 10, 11, 12, 70

secondary voltage 53, 54

sections 22, 37, 47, 81, 114, 115, 117

Security 106, 124

seed pods 6, 8

Seismic 115

Sensors 79, 88, 92

Service Visits 2, 3, 8, 45

Shear walls 114

shrub 11, 14, 15

shut-off 31, 32, 37, 40, 82, 99, 100, 101

shut-off valve 31, 32, 37, 40, 99

Shutters 123

Sidewall Head 80

Sills 92, 94, 96

sliding glass 108, 117, 123, 124

Snaking 122

soil-borne diseases 14

Solids 120, 121

Spalling 115, 119

Speed 33, 34, 35, 87, 88, 92, 93, 106

Printed in the United States
By Bookmasters